Risk Management Reimagined

A practical guide to cost control and safety excellence

By Jiles Smith II

First edition

ISBN: 978-1-967055-15-9

Published by Isham Media Group LLC
Temecula, California

"Most organizations don't care much about risk management, until something happens".

By Jiles Smith II

Dedication

In loving memory of my children, Dr. Lamar Smith and Ursula Martin Smith, who left this world far too soon.

Your time here was brief, but your impact is eternal. Your laughter once filled our home, your smiles lit our days, and your presence brought a joy that can never be replaced. Though you are no longer with us in body, your spirits live on in the memories we cherish and in the love that surrounds us always.

To my children who have gone ahead, you are deeply missed, forever cherished, and eternally loved. Your light will never fade, and your legacy lives in the lives you touched and the hearts you filled.

With love and remembrance,

Jiles Smith II

Preface

Why This Book Exists

Every organization faces risk.

Some treat it like a box to check. Others live in a constant state of worry, reacting from one crisis to the next. A few, though, begin to see risk as something deeper: a reflection of how people think, lead, communicate, and learn together.

This book is for that third group, and for those who want to join them.

Risk Management Reimagined is written for leaders, risk professionals, safety coordinators, and public-sector decision-makers who want more than compliance. You want workplaces that anticipate problems instead of waiting for them, that protect people and public trust, and that use resources wisely without burning out the people who keep everything running.

Drawing from decades of work in risk consulting, safety, governance, workers' compensation, and fraud prevention, this book blends real cases with a simple conviction:

- Resilience starts with people, not paperwork.

Policies matter. So do forms, audits, and dashboards. But they only work when they are grounded in clear thinking, honest conversations, and consistent follow-through. That is the work ahead.

How the Book Is Organized

The book is built in six connected parts. You can read it straight through or move to the sections that match where your organization is right now.

Part I – Foundations of Modern Risk Management

We start by reframing what risk management actually means today. You'll explore how to build strategies that balance legal requirements with real-world practicality and protect your organization from the silent drains of fraud, waste, and abuse. This section lays the groundwork: clear definitions, sound systems, and the connection between risk, cost, and culture.

Part II – The Human Core of Safety and Culture

Here we move from systems to people. This part examines how safety culture develops, how labels and language shape behavior, and how leaders can foster psychological safety while still holding people accountable. The Safety Cultural Competence Continuum (SC^3) gives you a way to see where your organization is today and how to move forward. You'll also see how time pressure, short-term decisions, and poor communication quietly erode safety from within.

Part III – Governance and Leadership

Structure matters. Who the risk manager reports to, how long people stay in key roles, and how leadership handles crises all shape your results. This section examines reporting lines, role rotation, retention, and succession planning. It also looks at crisis leadership and crisis management: how leaders can prepare before an event, stay steady during one, and learn honestly afterward.

Part IV – Data, Technology, and Human Decision-Making

Technology can either clarify risk or bury it under noise. In this part, we examine how data systems, analytics, and artificial intelligence can support better decision-making when used wisely. We also turn to behavioral economics to understand how real people actually decide under pressure. The message is simple: tools help, but people still make the final call.

Part V – Strategy, Sustainability, and Global Integration

This section widens the lens. It links sustainability, ethics, global trends, and social responsibility to everyday risk decisions. You'll see why organizations that think beyond the next quarter are not just "doing the right thing," but building long-term resilience. Topics include climate and ESG risk, global supply chain considerations, and what it means to lead with purpose in a changing world.

Part VI – Implementation, Measurement, and the Future

Finally, we turn vision into practice. You'll learn how to measure what truly matters, how to align safety and cost control without turning either into a hollow slogan, and how to give risk management a real seat at the table. We'll look at continuous improvement, ROI in safety, the forces that quietly destroy safety cultures, and how to keep risk conversations honest in a political and resource-constrained environment.

Taken together, these parts form a single argument: risk management should not live in a silo. It should be woven into strategy, leadership, budgeting, operations, and culture.

A Personal Note

My perspective on risk did not come from a single job or title. It evolved over years of sitting at different tables, seeing the same patterns appear in different clothes.

I've served as a California State Workers' Compensation Fraud Commissioner under two governors, watching how fraud, waste, and abuse distort a system meant to heal. I've worked with Fortune 500 companies, cities, school districts, joint powers authorities, and public agencies across the state and beyond. I've been in rooms where safety was treated as a distraction from "real work," and in others where leaders made safety and risk management central to their mission and saw everything else improve as a result.

I've seen what happens when near-misses are ignored, when people are afraid to speak up, and when culture is treated as an afterthought instead of the foundation. I've also seen how quickly things can change when leaders decide that safety is not just a priority, but a condition of employment and a measure of excellence.

Those experiences convinced me of three things:

1. Risk management is not only about avoiding lawsuits or satisfying regulators. It is about protecting people and public trust.

2. Culture will always beat paperwork. You can't write a policy strong enough to overcome a culture that doesn't mean it.

3. Good risk work saves money. Done well, it reduces claims, downtime, turnover, and costly surprises. Done poorly, it turns those costs into a permanent line item.

This book is my attempt to put those lessons in one place.

Jiles Smith II

The Path Forward

As you move through these chapters, I invite you to think about risk management in a different way.

Not as:

- a department that owns all the problems
- a set of forms to complete before something can move forward
- a cost center that only shows up in the budget as "insurance"

But as an organizational philosophy that belongs to everyone.

Every decision from the boardroom to the job site either strengthens resilience or quietly weakens it. The goal is not perfection. You will still have incidents, surprises, and bad days. The goal is progress:

- Systems that are failure-informed, not pretending to be failure-proof
- Cultures that encourage questions, not silence
- Leaders who see safety and cost control as partners, not opponents

This book is both a guide and a challenge:

- A guide, because it gives you tools, case examples, frameworks, and practical steps.
- A challenge, because it asks you to rethink who is responsible for risk and what you reward in your organization.

If you use these chapters only to polish existing reports, not much will change. If you use them to start new conversations, to question old habits, and to give your risk and safety people real support, you may find that "risk management" stops being something people avoid and starts becoming something they are proud to be part of.

There is a quote I return to often:

"Most organizations don't care much about risk management, until something happens."

My hope is that, by the time you finish this book, your organization will be one of the few that cares before something happens.

Jiles Smith II

TABLE OF CONTENTS

Part I: Foundation of Modern Risk Management

Chapter 1
Risk and Safety Assessments

Foundations for a Resilient Future

Introduction: More Than Paperwork

Most organizations can honestly say they "do" risk and safety assessments. There are inspection checklists, job hazard analyses, walkthrough forms, and sometimes even a risk matrix tucked into a policy binder or shared drive. On the surface, the tools exist.

And yet the same patterns keep showing up. Near misses go unreported. Incidents repeat. Loss runs start to look like a rerun: the same departments, the same causes, the same injuries and claims.

In many organizations, the problem is not the absence of tools. It is that the tools are treated like proof of effort rather than instruments for better decisions. A form gets completed, filed, and forgotten. A checklist is used once, usually after something goes wrong. A risk register gets built during a planning session and is never touched again.

This chapter reframes risk and safety assessments as a system, not a stack of templates. Modern risk frameworks, such as ISO 31000, describe risk assessment as part of an ongoing cycle: identify, analyze, evaluate, treat, and review risk over time (International Organization for Standardization [ISO], 2018). In other words, assessment is not the finish line. It is the start of responsible action.

When you look at assessments this way, the questions change. You stop asking, "Did we fill out the form?" and start asking:

- What decision is this assessment meant to support?

- Who will act on the result, and by when?

- What will we measure to know whether the control actually helped?

Those questions are where resilience begins.

Why Risk and Safety Assessments Matter

Risk and safety assessments live at the intersection of compliance, cost, and culture. That is why they matter so much.

From a compliance standpoint, assessments demonstrate that an organization understands its hazards and takes them seriously. Whether you are dealing with hazard identification, lockout/tagout, confined space entry, vehicle operations, or workplace violence prevention, regulators expect you to demonstrate a thoughtful process for identifying hazards and selecting controls. Assessments are often the most practical and defensible way to do that.

From a financial standpoint, assessments generate the information that should drive budgeting, resource allocation, and cost control. If a risk register shows that most severe incidents are connected to a small set of tasks or locations, then capital dollars and training time can be focused where they actually matter. Good assessments become early warning systems for future costs.

From a cultural standpoint, assessments send a message to employees about what leadership really values. When supervisors and leaders show up in the field, ask good questions, and follow through, employees notice. When assessments feel like an administrative chore that exists mainly to protect management after the fact, employees notice that too. Over time, people learn whether speaking up helps or creates more work with no change.

When assessments are done well, supervisors gain a clearer view of risk in their operations, frontline workers see their expertise reflected in procedures and improvements, and leaders get usable intelligence about where controls are weakening.

When assessments are done poorly, forms are completed after the job, hazards get reduced to vague labels like "unsafe behavior," and nothing changes. In that environment, people stop taking the process seriously because they are not being irrational. They are learning from experience.

The goal of this chapter is to help you move from "forms completed" to "risks reduced."

Four Families of Risk and Safety Assessment Tools

There are dozens of models and branded tools, but in day-to-day risk work, most approaches fall into four practical families:

1. Task-focused tools

2. Scoring and prioritization tools

3. System and barrier-focused tools

4. Culture and climate tools

Thinking in families keeps things simple. It helps you choose the right tool for the right job and combine tools into a coherent process (ISO, 2018).

Task-Focused Tools: Seeing the Hazards in the Work

Task-focused tools break work into steps, identify hazards at each step, and document controls. Job Hazard Analyses (JHAs) and Job Safety Analyses (JSAs) are common examples.

A simple task, such as loading materials into a truck, can be broken into steps: approach the vehicle, lift and place the load, and secure it. Each step has hazards, such as struck-by exposures, overexertion, pinch points, slips, and unstable loads. The value is not in the document. The value is in seeing the work clearly enough to reduce unnecessary risk.

Task-focused tools tend to be strongest when you use them:

- Before a new process or piece of equipment goes into service

- After an incident or near miss, to pinpoint where breakdowns occurred

- For high-frequency tasks where small changes add up to real savings over time

In many public-sector environments, routine tasks (clearing storm drains, repairing potholes, setting up facilities, maintaining parks) can quietly drive a large portion of injuries and minor vehicle incidents. These may not feel "major" in isolation, but they create a steady drain through strains, sprains, and repeated minor incidents.

Where organizations go wrong is predictable. They complete a JHA once and never revisit it. They fill it out in an office instead of at the worksite. They leave out the people who actually do the job, which reduces accuracy and signals that the organization does not value real expertise.

When task-focused tools are done right, they become a structured conversation with workers, not paperwork done to them. That conversation is where the most helpful information usually lives.

Scoring and Prioritization Tools: Separating Noise from Signal

Scoring tools help answer a practical question: With limited resources, where do we focus first?

Risk matrices, risk registers, and Failure Modes and Effects Analysis (FMEA) are common examples. These tools rate risk by likelihood and impact, sometimes adding detectability or other factors. Done well, they produce priorities that leadership can actually act on.

These tools are especially helpful during budgeting cycles and program planning. They allow leaders to compare risks that otherwise compete for attention based on whoever is loudest or whatever went wrong most recently.

One important point: the value is not mathematical precision. The numbers are a structured way to capture informed judgment. The real payoff is the discussion of the scoring forces, like:

- Do we truly agree this risk is "medium"?

- What evidence supports that rating?

- What would have to change for this risk to move up or down?

Common missteps include treating scores as permanent facts, clustering everything in the middle, and failing to update the register when conditions change or controls improve.

Used thoughtfully, scoring tools help organizations move from reactive decision-making to risk-based prioritization.

System and Barrier-Focused Tools: Looking at the Whole System

Some risks do not fail because of one mistake. They fail because multiple defenses weaken at the same time.

System and barrier tools shift the conversation away from "who messed up" and toward "how did the system allow this to happen." Bowtie analysis and barrier analysis are good examples. The Swiss Cheese Model, often used to explain layered defenses, is another common way to visualize how incidents occur when weaknesses line up across multiple layers (Reason, 1997).

A bowtie analysis starts with a central event, such as a serious fall, vehicle collision, chemical release, or violent incident. On the left, you map threats that could lead to the event. On the right, you map consequences. Between threats and the event, you document preventive controls, and between the event and consequences, you document mitigative controls.

These tools are especially useful for high-severity, low-frequency risks and for situations that require cross-department coordination. They are also useful after serious incidents, when leaders want to understand how multiple small problems combined into one big failure.

The most common mistake is building diagrams that look impressive but never get used again. Another is making them so complicated that no one can use them during real operations. A third is focusing only on technical controls and ignoring human and organizational contributors like staffing levels, training quality, fatigue, supervision, and communication (Hollnagel, 2014).

When used well, system tools reinforce a truth that strong organizations accept: no single control is perfect. Resilience comes from layers of defense, maintained over time.

Culture and Climate Tools: Measuring What People Really Experience

Culture tools focus on how people experience the organization. Surveys, focus groups, and structured listening sessions help you understand whether employees feel safe reporting hazards, whether supervisors follow through, and whether policies are viewed as realistic or something to work around.

These tools are particularly valuable:

- Before launching major initiatives, to establish a baseline

- After major changes in leadership, structure, or staffing

- Every couple of years, to measure trends over time

Culture assessments can backfire when mishandled. If you collect input and do nothing with it, trust drops. If questions are too vague, results are hard to translate into action. If culture is treated as separate from operational and financial performance, leaders miss the point.

Modern safety thinking emphasizes that safety is not only the absence of incidents but the presence of conditions that allow work to go right every day (Hollnagel, 2014). Culture tools help you see whether those conditions exist in reality.

Choosing the Right Tool for the Decision

A practical way to simplify tool selection is to start with the decision.

Instead of asking, "Which tool is best?" ask, "What decision are we trying to make?"

If you are designing a new program for powered industrial equipment, you likely need task-focused tools to capture routine hazards and system-level tools to address catastrophic scenarios like rollovers, pedestrian strikes, and overhead hazards.

If you are preparing a budget proposal, scoring tools help prioritize investments, and culture tools can reveal whether supervision, workload, or training gaps are undermining controls.

If you are responding to a serious near miss, task-focused tools help reconstruct what happened, system tools help explain how conditions aligned, and culture tools help answer a harder question: why did it take a near miss for this issue to surface?

Mature programs do not try to use every tool everywhere. They use a small core toolkit consistently and adjust only when there is a clear reason.

Common Pitfalls in Assessments

Even good organizations fall into predictable traps.

One is form over function. People complete documents because they are required, without learning anything from the process. In worse cases, assessments are created after an incident to make it look like the organization was prepared.

Another is the one-and-done mindset. An assessment gets done during a project phase and is never revisited, even as conditions change.

Another is siloed ownership. Safety owns the form, operations owns the work, and the assessment never fully reflects reality.

Another is the missing feedback loop. Workers share ideas and concerns, then see no visible response. Over time they stop engaging.

A final pitfall is ignoring weak signals. Near misses, small injuries, and recurring complaints are easy to dismiss, but many serious events are preceded by weak signals that were missed or dismissed.

These pitfalls are not fixed by better templates. They are fixed by better habits, clearer accountability, and stronger follow-through.

Building an Integrated Assessment Program

A practical way to strengthen your approach is to build in phases. This prevents the common mistake of trying to overhaul everything at once.

Phase 1: Clarify Purpose and Scope

Start with purpose. Are you trying to meet regulatory expectations, reduce claim costs, improve culture, or all three? Most organizations want all three, but the driver matters because it shapes tool selection and measurement.

Then identify your highest-risk operations. You do not need to fix everything at once. Start where the risk is real and visible enough to build momentum.

Phase 2: Select a Core Toolkit

Many organizations can build a strong foundation with:

- One or two task-focused tools (JHAs/JSAs and a simple inspection form)

- One prioritization tool (a basic risk matrix and risk register)

- One system-level tool (bowtie analysis for complex, high-hazard work)

- One culture tool (a short survey or structured listening sessions)

The goal is not sophistication. It is shared clarity about what tools are standard, when to use them, and how results will be applied.

Phase 3: Set Expectations and Train

Tool selection alone does not change outcomes. Supervisors, leads, and key frontline staff need practical training that focuses on how to think in the field, not how to fill out forms.

Training should help people distinguish hazards, risks, and controls, and recognize human and organizational contributors, not just technical issues.

Also, align performance expectations. If people are judged only on completion counts, they will optimize for volume over quality. If you measure quality and follow-through, the work becomes more meaningful.

Phase 4: Link Findings to KPIs and Decisions

Assessment findings should show up where decisions get made: capital planning, training plans, staffing conversations, and operational priorities.

A few practical leading indicators include corrective actions closed on time, completion of high-risk task assessments, and near-miss reporting trends.

Linking findings to KPIs moves assessments out of the safety silo and into normal management conversations.

Phase 5: Review, Learn, and Adjust

At least annually, step back and ask:

- Which tools are we actually using?

- What decisions are they influencing?

- Which risks are trending up, down, or holding steady?

- Where are people still going through the motions?

This review aligns with the continuous improvement cycle emphasized in ISO 31000 (ISO, 2018). Safety is not a static target. It is a living system that needs upkeep (Hollnagel, 2014).

Case Example: Turning Assessments into Savings

Consider a mid-sized public agency that saw a repeating pattern of strains and sprains among field staff. JHAs existed, but many were outdated and written in generic terms that did not reflect how work was actually being performed after equipment and staffing changes.

The agency took a targeted approach. Supervisors and safety staff re-did task analyses in the field, with crews walking through tasks step by step. They used a simple risk matrix to prioritize tasks based on frequency and potential severity. Instead of launching a large initiative, they tested small equipment and method changes in a few high-priority tasks.

They tracked incident rates, lost time, overtime, and feedback from crews over the next two years. Lost-time claims connected to the targeted tasks dropped, overtime tied to injury coverage decreased, and employees reported feeling heard. The tools were not complicated. The difference was consistent use and visible follow-through.

Conclusion: The Foundation Beneath Everything Else

Risk and safety assessments are the base layer for everything that follows in this book.

Strategic planning depends on knowing what risks truly matter. Culture work depends on understanding how people experience the system, not how it looks on paper. Technology and analytics depend on good inputs. Sustainability, governance, and ROI all rest on a clear picture of the risk landscape.

If assessments are shallow, everything built on top of them will wobble. If you strengthen this foundation even modestly, you gain leverage across your entire program.

A simple way to close this chapter with your team is to ask one question:

"If we could improve only one part of our assessment process this year, what change would have the biggest impact?"

Start there. Let the tools serve the conversation, not replace it.

References

Hollnagel, E. (2018). *Safety-I and Safety-II: The past and future of safety management.* CRC Press.

International Organization for Standardization. (2018). *ISO 31000:2018 risk management – Guidelines.* ISO.

Reason, J. (2016). *Managing the risks of organizational accidents.* Routledge.

Chapter 2
Cost Control Fundamentals in Risk Management

Understanding the Real Drivers of Loss, Frequency, and Severity

Cost Control Fundamentals

You cannot manage what you do not measure, and you cannot control cost without understanding what actually drives it. Losses have both direct and indirect costs, and the indirect side of the ledger often quietly exceeds what shows up in official reports. Frequency, severity, and exposure form the core math of cost control across workers' compensation, liability, auto, and property programs. Safety and cost control appear to conflict only when leaders treat them as separate goals rather than as two sides of the same decision. Simple, consistent metrics tied to real actions will move cost more than complex models that no one uses.

In almost every discussion about risk management, the conversation eventually comes back to a familiar question: "What is this costing us?"

Sometimes it comes from a city manager looking at rising workers' compensation reserves. Sometimes it is a finance director trying to explain liability trends. Sometimes it is a council member asking why premiums went up again. The pressure is real. But the bigger issue is this: most people can see the numbers, while far fewer understand the story behind those numbers.

Cost is not just a line on a spreadsheet. It is a narrative about how often things go wrong, how bad they are when they do, how long the organization stays off balance, and how many people and processes are quietly pulled off track along the way. When we reduce costs to a few dollar figures, we lose the patterns and decisions that created those numbers in the first place.

This chapter is about learning to read that story. We will look at the true cost of loss (what appears on reports and what does not), the basic mathematics of frequency and severity, key cost drivers in common public-entity risk programs, and how to connect safety and financial performance so they reinforce each other rather than compete for attention. By the end, cost control should feel less like guessing and more like a disciplined way to understand and change organizational patterns.

The True Cost of Loss

Most organizations can identify their direct loss costs. They can point to workers' compensation medical and indemnity payments, liability settlements, and legal defense expenses. These costs are visible because they flow through claims systems, invoices, and budget lines.

However, direct costs are only one part of the picture. Beneath the surface lie indirect costs that rarely appear in claims systems but absolutely impact finances and performance. Think about overtime to cover absent workers, reduced productivity while teams adjust, supervisor time spent on investigations and hearings, delayed projects, equipment downtime, onboarding replacement workers, and morale damage when people feel unsafe or unsupported.

National safety and labor organizations commonly note that indirect costs can be several times higher than direct costs (AFL-CIO, 2024; National Safety Council [NSC], 2025; Occupational Safety and Health Administration [OSHA], n.d.). When leadership focuses only on direct claim costs, it often underestimates both the true impact of incidents and the return on prevention.

Here is a practical way to make it real. Pick one significant claim from the last two years. List every direct cost you can see. Then sit with supervisors and ask: Who covered the work? What slipped? How many meetings, emails, and calls did this generate? What did we postpone because of this? You will quickly see why cost control cannot be reduced to settlement amounts, and why prevention usually has a stronger business case than it seems at first glance.

The Basic Math

Cost control rests on three interconnected concepts: frequency, severity, and exposure.

Frequency is how often events occur. Severity is the cost of each event when it occurs. Exposure is the opportunity for an event to occur, such as the number of employees, miles driven, calls for service, or public interactions.

A simplified way to think about it is:

Total Cost ≈ Frequency × Severity × Exposure

You will never control all three perfectly, but you can influence each in meaningful ways. Reducing frequency is a form of prevention: training, work design, safer surfaces, lifting practices, and enforced policies. Reducing severity is limiting harm when incidents occur: seat belts, fall protection, PPE, emergency response, early reporting, strong medical management, and return-to-work practices. Managing exposure is understanding where your risk lives so you can compare performance fairly over time and focus attention where it matters most.

Many organizations unintentionally overfocus on one side. Some celebrate lower counts while ignoring severity. Others react to a few big cases and ignore the steady drip of "smaller" losses that add up over time. A mature program watches both and makes resource decisions based on patterns, not emotions.

Where the Money Actually Goes

Different lines of coverage behave differently, but the most common cost drivers repeat across public-sector and service organizations.

Workers' Compensation

Workers' comp is often one of the largest controllable cost centers. The usual drivers include strains and sprains from lifting and awkward postures, slips, trips, and falls, vehicle-related injuries, and violence or aggression in public-facing environments.

But costs are shaped not only by the injury. Delayed reporting and delayed treatment can turn manageable injuries into expensive claims. The quality of medical care and coordination can shorten or extend disability. Return-to-work options can dramatically affect indemnity. Supervisor response and communication influence trust and disputes. Two employees can have similar injuries and create very different total costs based on what happens after the incident.

Liability

Liability losses often have fewer claims than workers' comp, but individual cases can be far more expensive. Common drivers include poor documentation, inconsistent enforcement, training gaps around conduct or de-escalation, vehicle policy failures, and contract language that shifts risk back to the agency.

Employment-related claims can be especially expensive, and they often reflect deeper cultural issues. If you only treat them as a legal problem, you usually miss the operational and leadership drivers that created the exposure.

Property and Infrastructure

Property losses tend to cluster around fire and water damage, aging infrastructure and deferred maintenance, and natural events exploiting known vulnerabilities. Preventive maintenance and resilient design can cost money up front, but they often pay back by reducing both frequency and severity over time.

Budgeting and Forecasting

Many organizations treat risk-related costs as something that "happens" to them. Premiums are seen as fixed. Claims are "unpredictable." Reserves are left to auditors and actuaries.

In reality, you have more influence than you think. Basic cost control starts with a clear trend-based picture of loss history. That usually means looking at three to five years of trends by line, department, cause, and severity band, plus open inventory and how losses develop over time.

You don't need to be an actuary to use data well. Actuaries estimate future obligations based on patterns. Your job is to connect the patterns back to real work and ask: What in our operations is creating these trends? Which drivers can we realistically influence in the next 12 to 24 months?

When you present budget requests tied directly to loss trends and projected savings, risk management stops looking like overhead and starts looking like strategy.

Aligning Cost Control With Safety

There is a persistent myth: "Safety costs money. Cost control means cutting."

That myth creates a tug-of-war between safety and finance. In practice, uncontrolled loss is usually far more expensive than prevention. The timing is what tricks people. Prevention costs are immediate and visible this year. Loss costs are delayed and scattered across years.

Leaders need a way to compare trade-offs clearly. Flooring improvements and housekeeping reduce falls and the hidden costs that follow. Driver training and telematics reduce collisions and third-party claims. A structured modified-duty program reduces wage-replacement costs and keeps employees connected to work and routine.

The questions leaders should be asking sound like normal investment questions: What losses are we likely to avoid over five years? What non-financial benefits do we gain? How will we measure whether it worked?

When you frame cost control as protecting people and dollars at the same time, the conversation shifts from "Can we afford this?" to "Can we afford not to?"

Practical Metrics and KPIs

Metrics don't have to be complicated to be powerful. The best metrics are simple, understood by non-specialists, and tied to action.

Standard cost-control metrics include total cost of risk, cost per claim, frequency rates normalized by exposure, severity indicators (such as the concentration of cost in the top claims), and open-claim inventory with aging.

To keep metrics useful, start with a small set for senior leaders. Combine cost, frequency, and severity. Clearly separate lagging indicators from leading indicators. Include prevention metrics like corrective actions closed on time or completion of high-risk task assessments.

Every metric on a dashboard should answer one question: If this moves in the wrong direction, what are we prepared to do?

Common Mistakes in Cost Control

Organizations tend to fall into a few predictable traps.

One is chasing short-term savings by cutting training, deferring maintenance, or shrinking prevention efforts. That might reduce this year's spending, but it often increases future loss (OSHA, n.d.; NSC, 2025). Another is focusing only on big, rare events while ignoring the steady accumulation of moderate losses that cost more over time.

A third mistake is treating cost control as "risk's job" or "finance's job." Costs are created and prevented where the work happens, so the people closest to operations must be part of the conversation. Another trap is measuring without acting. Beautiful dashboards do not change outcomes unless they drive real decisions. Finally, if you ignore human factors such as trust and fairness, you may inadvertently encourage underreporting or working through pain, which can increase severity and long-term costs.

Case Examples: What Cost Control Looks Like in Real Life

Example 1: The "Small Claims" Problem That Was not Small

A mid-sized city continued to see a steady flow of medical-only workers' comp claims. Nothing dramatic. A strained back here, a sore shoulder there, a few slips that did not become lost-time cases. Leadership assumed it was normal wear and tear, the kind of thing you live with in public works and facilities. On paper, each claim looked manageable.

When the risk team pulled 24 months of data and grouped it by task, the pattern got clearer. The same few jobs were responsible for most of the reports: moving trash bins, loading equipment, repetitive lifting of supplies, and awkward reaching in storage areas. The real cost was not just medical bills. It was the chain reaction. Extra breaks because someone was stiff. Overtime to keep routes and service levels up. Supervisors are losing hours each week to paperwork and check-ins. A few experienced employees quietly avoid certain tasks, which shifts the burden to newer staff.

Instead of launching a big "safety campaign," the city treated it like process improvement. They changed storage layouts to reduce high reaches and deep bends, replaced a few worn carts and dollies, standardized how crews staged materials before jobs, and required supervisors to do short walk-throughs on high-frequency tasks. Within a year, the number of new claims tied to those tasks dropped noticeably. More importantly, the department stopped bleeding time. The city didn't "eliminate injuries." They reduced a costly pattern that had become routine.

Example 2: Return to Work as the Difference Between a Claim and a Crisis

A school district had a handful of claims each year that seemed to explode in cost. The injuries varied, but the ending was often the same: extended time away, frustration on both sides, and a slow drift into litigation or permanent restrictions. The district's leaders kept asking the same question: "Why are we paying so much for a few cases?"

The review uncovered a simple operational issue. The district had no consistent modified duty process, and supervisors were improvising. Some employees were kept off work entirely because it was "easier." Others returned without clear limits, exacerbating the injury. In several cases, the employee's absence created staffing shortages that led to overtime and increased burnout, which in turn increased the risk of subsequent injury.

The fix was not complicated, but it required discipline. HR, risk, and department leadership built a short list of realistic transitional tasks that actually needed to be done. They trained supervisors on how to use restrictions as guardrails, not as reasons to sideline someone. They also set a timeline expectation: contact within 24 hours, early medical coordination, and weekly check-ins with a consistent script that kept the tone supportive yet clear.

The result was less time off work, fewer disputes, and lower indemnity exposure. Even when medical costs stayed similar, the claim totals dropped because the disability portion shrank. The district learned a hard truth that applies everywhere: many claims become expensive not because the injury was extreme, but because the organization lost control of the "after."

Example 3: Liability Costs Driven by Documentation, Not Just Incidents

A city's liability claims were not constant, but when they hit, they hit hard. Several were slip-and-fall claims in public areas, and a few were auto-related third-party claims. Leadership wanted to buy new equipment and add training, but the risk manager pushed for a different first step: look at how claims were defended.

The review found that the organization often could not tell a clean story. Maintenance logs were inconsistent. Photos were rarely taken. Citizen complaints were not tracked in a way that connected to corrective action. In a few cases, the city had done the right things operationally but could not prove it, so settlements became the least bad option.

The city treated documentation as part of the control environment rather than a bureaucratic requirement. They simplified how crews recorded inspections and repairs, established a basic photo practice for specific exposures, and standardized the logging and routing of complaints. They also trained supervisors on what to capture when an incident occurred, not through a long lecture but through a short, practical playbook.

Within a year, claims did not disappear, but outcomes improved. Some cases were resolved faster because the facts were clearer. Others were denied or defended more effectively because the city could demonstrate reasonable care. In liability, cost control often comes down to whether you can show you acted responsibly, consistently, and on time.

Example 4: Fleet Losses and the "One Bad Week" Illusion

A county department saw a spike in auto losses and assumed it was a short-term "bad luck" run. A couple of backing incidents. A side swipe. A minor collision at an intersection. Nothing catastrophic, but enough to raise questions and trigger pressure from finance.

When they looked more closely, the collisions were clustered around two factors: rushed routes and poor backing practices at job sites. The department's service expectations had quietly increased, but vehicle operations had not been adjusted to match the reality. Drivers were making decisions under time pressure, and supervisors were rewarding speed without realizing the risk signal they were sending.

The department changed a few habits. They updated route-planning expectations so that "on time" did not mean "unsafe fast." They implemented a simple backing rule that required spotters in specific situations, and they made it normal for supervisors to ask about vehicle hazards during routine check-ins. They also used incident reviews as learning conversations, not punishment sessions, so drivers reported near misses and hazards earlier.

The improvements showed up in two places: fewer claims and fewer work disruptions. Auto losses are not just about repair bills. They bring downtime, schedule breakdowns, and reputational damage. When fleet risk is treated as operational risk rather than "driver error," the numbers usually follow.

Example 5: Deferred Maintenance That Turned Into Predictable Loss

A facilities division had been deferring maintenance for years. Everyone understood why. Budgets were tight, staffing was short, and there were always more urgent problems. But the organization started seeing a rising pattern of property and equipment losses: water damage from plumbing failures, HVAC breakdowns during heat waves, and electrical issues that caused downtime and emergency vendor calls.

The cost control problem wasn't only the repairs. It was the emergency nature of the work. Emergency vendors were more expensive. Repairs happened after hours. Critical spaces were impacted, creating disruptions that affected operations far beyond the facility team.

Instead of trying to fix everything, leadership prioritized the systems that created the most disruption and loss when they failed. They created a small preventive maintenance plan focused on the highest consequence assets and set realistic service standards that reflected staffing. They also tracked repeat failures and used them to justify targeted capital requests.

Over time, fewer failures became emergencies. Costs became more predictable. This is one of the clearest examples of cost control you can show a finance audience: planned work is almost always cheaper than crisis work, and it protects operations while it saves money.

Conclusion

Cost control in risk management isn't about saying no to everything that costs money. It's about understanding where and why money is leaving the organization and making deliberate choices to change those patterns.

When leaders can clearly see the full cost of loss, the basic math of frequency severity and exposure, the cost drivers across workers' comp and liability, and how prevention investments pay off over time, cost control stops being a guessing game. It becomes a shared responsibility woven into daily decision-making.

In the next chapter, we'll look at another force that quietly erodes both cost and trust: fraud, waste, and abuse.

References

AFL-CIO. (2024). *Death on the job: The toll of neglect.* AFL-CIO.

National Safety Council. (2025). *Injury facts.* National Safety Council.

Occupational Safety and Health Administration. (n.d.). *$afety Pays: Background of cost estimates.* U.S. Department of Labor.

Chapter 3
Guarding the Gates

Fraud, Waste, and Abuse in Risk Programs

Guarding the Gates: Fraud, Waste, and Abuse in Risk Programs

Most organizations do not lose money to fraud, waste, and abuse in one loud scandal. They lose it quietly. A claim gets accepted with thin documentation because everyone is busy. A vendor invoice slides through because "they always do good work." A supervisor makes an exception to be helpful, and the exception becomes a habit. Then it becomes a pattern. Then it becomes a budget problem.

Fraud, waste, and abuse are not just ethics topics or audit topics. They are operational risks. They distort your loss data, inflate your total cost of risk, and create resentment inside the organization because people can feel when the system is being played. If you want cleaner outcomes in workers' compensation, liability, procurement, and vendor management, you need better gates. Not more bureaucracy. Better gates.

This chapter is about guarding those gates in a way that protects resources and protects trust, without turning leadership into a suspicion machine.

What We Mean by Fraud, Waste, and Abuse

Organizations use different terms, but the distinctions matter because they shape how you respond.

Fraud is intentional deception for an unauthorized benefit. That can show up as a knowingly false claim, falsified documentation, manipulated billing, or a deliberate attempt to shift cost onto a program that is not meant to cover it (Association of Certified Fraud Examiners [ACFE], 2024; U.S. Government Accountability Office [GAO], 2023).

Waste is the unnecessary use of resources due to poor management, inefficiency, weak oversight, or bad process design. Waste often is not criminal, but it is still a preventable loss.

Abuse sits in the uncomfortable middle. It is behavior that violates accepted standards and results in unnecessary cost or unfair advantage, even if the intent to deceive is less clear than fraud. Abuse often survives because it is tolerated, rationalized, or treated as too awkward to confront (Centers for Medicare & Medicaid Services [CMS], 2017; GAO, 2023).

A simple way to say it in a leadership meeting is: fraud is lying, abuse is bending, and waste is leaking. You may use different tools for each, but the same money disappears.

Why FWA Belongs in Risk Management

Risk management is supposed to protect people and protect the mission. Fraud, waste, and abuse hit both.

It increases cost directly through payments that never should have happened. It also increases cost indirectly by consuming time, clogging systems, and distorting the data you rely on to set priorities. When a claims program is polluted with questionable cases, you end up treating noise as a hazard trend. When procurement controls are weak, vendor pricing and change orders start to look "normal." When timekeeping abuse is tolerated, you carry the cost as if it were a staffing need.

FWA also breaks culture. People may not know all the details, but they notice patterns. They notice who gets exceptions. They notice whether reporting concerns leads to action or consequences. Over time, tolerance of FWA teaches the organization a corrosive lesson: rules are for some people, not for everyone.

For public agencies and public-facing organizations, there's a final layer. FWA is stewardship risk. When it becomes visible, it damages credibility in ways that are hard to repair.

Where Fraud, Waste, and Abuse Commonly Show Up

Claims and Benefits

Claims programs are attractive targets because they involve money, discretion, and emotion. Workers' compensation, liability claims, leave programs, accommodation decisions, and modified duty placements all create opportunities if gates are weak.

Some patterns are familiar across organizations:

Late reporting with thin detail, especially when the story is hard to verify.
Claims that escalate sharply over time without a clear medical explanation.
Repeated use of the same providers, attorneys, or referral networks that concentrate cost.
Modified duty that becomes indefinite and unproductive, framed as support but experienced by coworkers as unfairness.

Not every odd pattern is fraud. That matters. Your goal is not to accuse people. Your goal is to notice outliers, tighten documentation, and reduce opportunity for misuse.

Vendors, Procurement, and Contracting

Procurement is a high-value gate. It includes direct risk-related vendors like TPAs, investigators, nurse case managers, defense counsel, medical vendors, safety consultants, and training providers.

Weak points tend to repeat:

- Vague scopes of work that make invoices hard to challenge.
- Informal "preferred vendor" practices without periodic rebids or performance reviews.
- Change orders that quietly become the real contract.
- Relationships that create conflicts of interest, even when nobody calls it that out loud.

A practical truth is that procurement problems often begin as convenience. The organization is tired and busy, and the same vendor is easy. Convenience is not evil, but it needs controls.

Payroll, Timekeeping, and Vehicle Use

Payroll and fleet are high-frequency systems. That makes them perfect for low-level abuse that becomes expensive in aggregate. Overtime padding, questionable mileage, unauthorized vehicle use, and fuel misuse are rarely dramatic. They become costly because they repeat.

Program Design and Policy Loopholes

Some organizations unintentionally design programs that invite gamesmanship. Broad exceptions, vague criteria, and inconsistent enforcement create a system where the gate is not a gate at all. Tightening program design can reduce abuse without turning it into a personal confrontation. In many cases, the cleanest fix is to clarify criteria and document decisions consistently.

Who Commits It, and Why It's Hard to See

Occupational fraud research consistently shows that many cases involve insiders, not strangers. That matters because insiders understand your process better than you do, especially if no one has mapped it end-to-end (ACFE, 2024).

They know where steps are not checked, where approvals are rubber-stamped, and which supervisors avoid conflict. They also know the language of your system. That's why FWA can hide in plain sight.

The fraud triangle is still a useful lens here: pressure, opportunity, rationalization. You cannot manage everyone's personal pressures, but you can reduce opportunity through controls and reduce rationalization through consistent leadership behavior and fair accountability (ACFE, 2024).

This is where tone at the top becomes real. If leadership models exceptions, tolerates vendor gifts, looks away from favored employees, or handles similar cases differently based on politics, rationalization spreads.

A Practical Framework for Guarding the Gates

Most effective FWA programs rest on three pillars: prevention, detection, and response. You need all three. If one is missing, the whole effort becomes theater.

Prevention

Prevention is not about distrust. It's about system design.

Start with basic internal controls:

- Segregation of duties where possible, so one person does not control setup, approval, and payment.
- Clear criteria for decisions that create financial exposure, especially modified duty, leave approvals, and vendor selection.
- Conflict-of-interest disclosures that are not just collected, but reviewed.
- Training that uses real examples from your environment so people recognize red flags in their daily work.

Prevention is also about reducing discretion without eliminating it. You can keep human judgment in the system while still building guardrails.

Detection

Even well-designed controls miss things. Detection catches what leaks through.

Tips matter. Across many studies, tips are a leading source of detection. That means a reporting channel only works if people trust it and believe retaliation will not follow (ACFE, 2024).

Detection also includes basic monitoring that matches your size and capacity. You do not need an advanced analytics shop to make progress. You need consistent pattern checks, such as:

- Clusters of claims around predictable timing points.
- Unusual treatment utilization patterns.
- Repeat concentration around certain vendors, providers, or attorneys.
- Change order frequency and invoice patterns that drift beyond scope.
- Overtime patterns that are unusually consistent or poorly explained.
- Mileage and fuel patterns that do not align with routes or workload.

The mindset here matters. You are not trying to prove wrongdoing with a dashboard. You are trying to identify what deserves a second look.

Response

Response is where credibility is either built or destroyed.

If people see that leadership takes concerns seriously, investigates fairly, and follows through consistently, reporting increases and opportunity decreases. If people see favoritism, silence, or "we handled it quietly," the culture shifts toward cynicism.

A credible response framework usually includes:

- Clear intake and triage steps for allegations.
- Objective criteria for escalation and investigation.
- Proportionate consequences based on facts, not emotion or politics.
- Remediation of the control gap so the same pattern cannot repeat.
- High-level reporting to leadership on trends and corrective actions, without turning it into a public shaming exercise.

It is also important to distinguish honest error from abuse and fraud. If an organization treats mistakes as fraud, people will hide problems. That makes everything worse.

A Composite Case: The Exception That Became a System

A public agency begins seeing higher workers' compensation and leave costs within one division. The incident narratives look plausible. The people involved are known, and leadership wants to be supportive. Reporting is often late, documentation is thin, and modified duty assignments are informal and open-ended.

Nothing about it feels like a crime. It feels like compassion and flexibility.

Over time, the pattern grows. Coworkers start to complain quietly that the same people are always "on restrictions" and still collecting overtime. Supervisors stop questioning it because they don't want conflict. The risk team notices a concentration of costs and recurring friction points, but the organization lacks a consistent gate for modified-duty decisions, and no one wants to be the bad guy.

When leadership finally addresses it, the fix is not a dramatic fraud takedown. It is a reset of the gates:

- Clear criteria for transitional work.
- Time limits and weekly review.
- Documentation standards that apply to everyone.
- Supervisor coaching that teaches support without enabling.
- Simple monitoring so outliers are discussed early, not after costs explode.

In many organizations, that is what waste and abuse look like. Not villainy. Drift, avoidance, and weak gates.

Closing

Fraud, waste, and abuse are preventable drains on cost, trust, and credibility. The organizations that handle them well do not do it by assuming everyone is dishonest. They do it by designing systems that make honesty easier, make exceptions visible, and make accountability consistent.

Guarding the gates is a risk strategy. It protects the budget, it protects the integrity of your data, and it protects the people who are trying to do the right thing in a system that is often under pressure.

In the next chapter, we shift from guarding gates to shaping climate, the daily conditions that determine whether people speak up, follow through, and treat safety as real.

References

Association of Certified Fraud Examiners. (2024). *Occupational fraud 2024: A report to the nations.* ACFE.

Centers for Medicare & Medicaid Services. (2017). *Combating Medicare Parts C & D fraud, waste and abuse.* U.S. Department of Health and Human Services.

Community Health Plan of Washington. (2025). *Fraud, waste, and abuse.* Community Health Plan of Washington.

Kumaraswamy, N., Markey, M. K., Ekin, T., Barner, J. C., & Rascati, K. (2022). Healthcare fraud data mining methods: A look back and look ahead. *Perspectives in Health Information Management, 19*(1), 1i.

National Health Care Anti-Fraud Association. (n.d.). *The challenge of health care fraud.* NHCAA.

New Jersey Society of CPAs. (2024, September 20). *Preventing and detecting occupational fraud.* NJCPA.

U.S. Department of Justice. (2024, January 17). *2024 DOJ fraud section year in review.* U.S. Department of Justice.

U.S. Department of Justice. (2025, June 30). *Record-breaking $14.6 billion health care fraud takedown announced.* U.S. Department of Justice.

U.S. Government Accountability Office. (2023). *Improper payments and fraud: How they are related but different (GAO-24-106608).* GAO.

U.S. Government Accountability Office. (2025a, February 26). *GAO's high-risk list highlights ways to save billions and help agencies work better.* GAO.

U.S. Government Accountability Office. (2025b, March 11). *Improper payments: Information on agencies' fiscal year 2024 estimates (GAO-25-107753).* GAO.

Part II: People, Culture, and Safety

Chapter 4
The Safety Cultural Competence Continuum (SC^3)

Assessing and Advancing Your Culture

Assessing and Advancing Your Culture

Safety culture is not your posters, policies, or slogans. It is what people actually do when time is tight, and nobody is watching, and it shows up in both outcomes and costs. The same habits that lead to injuries, downtime, and claims often normalize small failures until they become big ones. If you want to improve culture, you have to see it clearly first, which means using more than a survey. You need a mix of data, observation, and honest conversations that make it safe for people to speak up early. The SC^3 continuum treats culture as a progression, not a switch, so leaders can name where they are today and choose practical next steps that actually stick.

Culture Is the Operating System

Most organizations can point to a safety manual, a training calendar, and a list of required inspections. Some can point to a safety committee and a good-looking dashboard. Yet the same injuries keep showing up, the same near misses keep getting "handled," and the same departments keep driving the loss runs.

That gap is rarely a paperwork problem. It is a culture problem.

Culture is the operating system of the workplace. It shapes what gets noticed, what gets reported, what gets fixed, and what gets quietly tolerated. Edgar Schein's work is still one of the cleanest ways to say it: culture is the shared assumptions that a group learns over time, and those assumptions show up in behavior because "this is how we do things here" (Schein, 2010). In safety, that means the real rules are often unwritten. They live in hallway conversations, in how supervisors react to bad news, and in whether "production first" is implied even when leaders say "safety first."

A strong safety culture is not soft. It is disciplined. It has standards, follow-through, and a learning posture. It is also honest about trade-offs, because the real world always brings pressure: staffing shortages, deadlines, public demand, aging equipment, and the temptation to cut corners "just this once."

This chapter gives you a practical way to see and strengthen culture using the Safety Cultural Competence Continuum (SC^3). The purpose is not to label people as good or bad. The purpose is to help leaders and risk professionals describe reality clearly enough to change it.

Culture vs. Climate: What You're Actually Measuring

You will hear both terms, sometimes used interchangeably.

Safety climate is often described as the "snapshot" of how employees perceive safety at a given time, shaped by what leaders are emphasizing right now (Zohar, 1980). Safety culture is deeper and more stable. It is the long-term pattern of assumptions, values, and norms that shape behavior (Schein, 2010). Climate can change quickly. Culture changes more slowly because it is reinforced by what gets rewarded, what gets ignored, and what people believe will happen if they speak up.

In practice, you need both lenses.

Climate tells you what people are experiencing today. Culture tells you why those experiences keep repeating.

A helpful warning: climate surveys can be useful, but they can also create harm if the organization collects feedback and then does nothing visible with it. That pattern teaches people that speaking up is pointless, which is the opposite of what you want.

The SC³ Model: A Continuum, Not a Slogan

The SC³ approach treats culture as a continuum with recognizable stages. Organizations can be in different stages at the same time across different departments. A city's fleet division might be relatively mature while parks operations is struggling. A hospital's surgical unit might have strong stop-the-line norms while environmental services has a fear-based reporting climate.

The goal is not to brag about being "advanced." The goal is to identify the next move that will actually stick.

Below are six stages that many organizations move through. The descriptions are intentionally concrete because culture becomes clearer when behaviors are described rather than intentions.

SAFETY CULTURAL COMPETENCY CONTINUUM MODEL

Components	Safety Cultural Destructiveness	Safety Cultural Incapacity	Safety Cultural Blindness	Safety Cultural Pre-Competence	Safety Cultural Competence	Safety Cultural Proficiency
Leadership Commitment to Safety	Disregard safety entirely, seeing it as a "cost of doing business."	Safety messaging is inconsistent and superficial	Assume all employees share the same safety values without actively reinforcing them.	Recognize the importance of safety but struggle to align it with operational goals.	Consistently emphasize safety as a core value.	Actively champion safety innovation and improvement.
Employee Involvement	Feedback is ignored, and dissenting voices are silenced.	Aware of safety policies but feel discouraged or powerless to contribute.	Follow safety procedures only to meet quotas. Safety feedback is solicited but not acted upon.	Encouraged to participate, but mechanisms for involvement are underdeveloped.	Actively participate in safety programs and provide regular feedback	Lead safety initiatives and mentor peers in safety best practices
Training and Competence	Non-existent or inadequate training on safety protocols	Exists but is outdated inconsistent, or irrelevant,	Generic and assumes all employees share the same safety needs	Programs developed but not fully integrated into operations.	Effectiveness is regularly evaluated and improved.	Dynamic, updated continuously, focus on emerging risks.
Accountability	No one is held accountable for unsafe practices.	Accountability measures are nonexistent, or selectively applied	Accountability is only addressed in response to major incidents	Accountability measures are introduced but not fully implemented.	Clear account-ability structures in place, performance regularly reviewed.	Embedded into the organization's culture, with shared outcome ownership
Communication	Safety communication is absent or actively suppressed.	Inconsistent or unclear messaging, sporadic and doesn't meet needs	Safety messages are generic and fail to address specific needs	Leaders begin to solicit feedback but struggle with follow-through	Consistent, clear, and emphasizes relevance to team	Fosters open dialogue, feedback and culture of trust
Measurement and Feedback	Safety performance is not measured at all.	Metrics are collected inconsistently or only for compliance.	Metrics focused solely on lagging indicators such as incident rates	Metrics are developed but no integration with operational goals	Data is used to drive improvements.	Feedback drives innovation and strategic planning.
Integration with Organizational Goals	Safety goals actively undermined to prioritize production.	Integration efforts are superficial or non-existent.	Safety in planning but not fully integrated operations	Safety included in planning but not consistently prioritized	Safety embedded into strategic and operational plans.	Core organizational value, fully integrated
Continuous Improvement	Resistant to change and perpetuates unsafe practices.	Improvements are reactive rather than proactive.	Change is seen as unnecessary or burdensome.	Initiatives are launched but inconsistently implemented.	Organizational priority with regular updates.	Model of safety excellence in its industry.

Modified from "The Cultural Competence Continuum" by Cross, T. L., Bazron, B. J., Isaacs, M. R.., & Dennis, K. W. (1989) in collaboration with Dr. Lamar Jerome Smith in 2014.

Safety Cultural Destructiveness: "We Don't Care and We Punish"

This stage is rare in modern organizations as an official stance, but it still appears in pockets.

What it looks like:

- Leaders dismiss injuries as weakness, bad luck, or "part of the job."

- Reporting is punished, directly or indirectly. People who report are labeled complainers.

- Shortcuts are celebrated. Safety rules are enforced only after something goes wrong.

- Blame is the default. Learning is not the goal. Protection of reputation is the goal.

Common signals:

- High underreporting and high severity when incidents finally surface.

- Repeated "surprise" events that were predictable to frontline staff.

- Turnover or disengagement among strong employees who don't want to operate in fear.

Leadership move that matters:
Stop the harm. Establish non-negotiables around retaliation, basic PPE, and the right to report hazards without punishment. This is not a "training" fix. It is a leadership and accountability fix.

Safety Cultural Incapacity: "We Mean Well, But We're Not Built for This"

In this stage, people may care, but the organization lacks structure and consistency.

What it looks like:

- Policies exist, but they are outdated, generic, or not integrated into operations.

- Supervisors are stretched and inconsistent. Safety depends on which boss you get.

- Training is reactive and checkbox-driven.

- Hazards are known, but corrective actions linger because nobody owns closure.

Common signals:

- Lots of activity, little reduction in repeat incidents.

- Audits identify the same gaps year after year.

- Safety is treated as an extra job, not part of the job.

Leadership move that matters:
Build capacity. Clarify roles, create a small set of standard expectations, and resource corrective action closure. If people are drowning, they will not build culture. They will survive the day.

Safety Cultural Blindness: "We Think We're Fine"

This is one of the most common and most dangerous stages, because the organization believes it is doing better than it is.

What it looks like:

- Leaders assume "common sense" covers safety.

- Safety messaging exists, but it is shallow and repetitive.

- Paperwork looks good, but it is not trusted.

- Low reporting is interpreted as "we don't have problems."

This is the stage where organizations often say, "We have a great safety culture," right before a serious incident.

Common signals:

- Low near-miss reporting, but recurring injuries.

- "We've always done it this way" logic in high-risk tasks.

- Risk is treated as a compliance issue rather than an operational reality.

Leadership move that matters:
Create visibility and humility. Leaders need better listening systems and better leading indicators. In practical terms: do field walk-throughs that focus on barriers and work constraints, not fault-finding (Reason, 1997). Ask: "What makes the safe way hard to do here?"

Safety Cultural Pre-Competence: "We See the Gap and We're Trying"

This stage is a turning point. The organization recognizes it needs to change and begins building discipline.

What it looks like:

- More deliberate training and communication.

- Leaders start asking for safety feedback and begin taking action on it.

- Safety metrics begin aligning with operational metrics.

- Documentation improves and becomes more realistic.

Common signals:

- A mix of cynicism and hope among employees.

- Increased reporting (which can temporarily make numbers look worse).

- Leaders are learning how to respond without blame.

Leadership move that matters:
Protect the momentum. This is where psychological safety becomes a real control. When people report more, leaders must respond consistently or the window closes (Edmondson, 1999). Early wins matter, especially around closing corrective actions and making visible changes.

Safety Cultural Competence: "We Do Safety on Purpose"

In this stage, safety is integrated into how work is planned, staffed, and executed.

What it looks like:

- Leaders treat safety as a condition of employment, not a motivational poster.

- Supervisors coach safety in the flow of work.

- Near misses and hazards are discussed openly and used for learning.

- Training connects to actual risk drivers, not generic topics.

Common signals:

- Stronger leading indicators: corrective actions closed, field observations that lead to fixes, participation in JHAs, improved maintenance response time.

- Fewer repeat incidents.

- Better trust between labor and management around safety issues.

Leadership move that matters:
Standardize what works. Capture the successful practices and make them the norm across departments. This is also where governance matters: who owns risk decisions, how priorities get funded, and how trade-offs are documented.

Safety Cultural Proficiency: "We Learn Fast and We Stay Humble"

This is not "perfect safety." It is mature safety.

What it looks like:

- Leaders and employees treat safety as a living system that can drift and must be maintained.

- People talk openly about weak signals.

- Learning is faster than blame.

- The organization invests in prevention because it understands the long game.

This stage aligns with modern thinking that safety is not only the absence of incidents, but the presence of conditions that help work go right consistently (Hollnagel, 2014).

Common signals:

- Strong speak-up culture, including respectful challenge upward.

- Consistent use of learning reviews after events, not just investigations.

- Improvements are sustained across leadership changes.

Leadership move that matters:
Keep the learning system alive. Organizations at this stage avoid complacency by continually checking drift, workload pressure, staffing strain, and the quality of supervision.

How to Assess Your Culture Without Fooling Yourself

A credible culture assessment is not one tool. It is triangulation. You are looking for consistent patterns across multiple sources.

Here are four practical inputs.

Operational data

Use your loss runs, injury logs, vehicle incident data, and general liability patterns. But do not stop at totals. Slice it:

- Frequency vs. severity

- Repeat causes

- Department and supervisor patterns

- Lag time from incident to report

- Litigation and dispute rates (which often reflect trust)

Numbers are not "the truth," but they often point to where the truth is hiding.

Leading indicators

Leading indicators are culture-sensitive. They show whether people are engaged and whether leaders follow through. Examples include:

- Corrective actions closed on time

- Quality of JHAs or JSAs (not just completion)

- Near-miss reporting volume and quality

- Safety meeting participation that includes real discussion

- Supervisor field coaching frequency

A key point: if your leading indicators are mostly "completed training" and "forms submitted," you are measuring activity, not culture.

Observation and listening

You learn culture by watching work and hearing the "why" behind it.

- Walk jobs with crews and ask what makes tasks hard.

- Ask where procedures do not match reality.

- Listen for normalized shortcuts and accepted drift.

This is where the Swiss Cheese reality shows up: serious incidents often result from the alignment of multiple minor weaknesses, not from a single bad decision (Reason, 1997).

Climate survey or pulse checks

Surveys can help, especially when paired with focus groups. Keep them practical. Ask about:

- Comfort reporting hazards

- Supervisor consistency

- Confidence in follow-through

- Fairness in accountability

- Workload pressure that pushes risk

Then do the most important part: close the loop. If you cannot act, do not ask.

The Hidden Engine: Psychological Safety and Speak-Up Culture

If you want fewer surprises, you need more truth earlier.

Amy Edmondson's research on psychological safety frames it as a shared belief that it is safe to take interpersonal risks, such as asking questions, admitting mistakes, or raising concerns (Edmondson, 1999). In risk terms, psychological safety is not a feel-good concept. It is an early-warning system. Without it, weak signals stay buried until the organization pays for them.

This is why leaders should treat "how we respond to bad news" as a risk control. If supervisors respond with sarcasm, anger, or public embarrassment, reporting will fall. If leaders respond with curiosity and follow-through, reporting becomes normal.

A practical standard for leaders: respond to reports in a way that makes the next report more likely.

Moving Up the Continuum: What Actually Changes Culture

Culture shifts when the daily incentives and daily frictions change. Here are the levers that matter most.

Leadership clarity and consistency

People believe what leaders consistently enforce, not what leaders occasionally say. If a supervisor is rewarded for speed and output while safety is treated as optional, the culture will follow the reward.

Consistency includes consequences. Not harshness, but fairness. A culture that tolerates repeated unsafe behavior from high performers teaches everyone that safety is negotiable.

Systems that make the safe way the easy way

If safe work requires extra steps, extra time, or extra hassle, people will drift. Engineering controls, equipment upgrades, realistic staffing, and maintenance response times all shape culture because they shape what is possible.

This is why culture work cannot be separated from budgeting. The budget is a values document.

Learning reviews that focus on causes, not scapegoats

When something goes wrong, the organization teaches itself either fear or learning. Use reviews that ask:

- What conditions made this outcome possible?
- What barriers failed or were missing?
- What pressures or constraints were present?
- What would prevent recurrence in the real world?

This aligns with "just culture" thinking, where accountability is real but not simplistic (Dekker, 2014).

Manager and supervisor capability

Most culture is built or destroyed at the supervisor level. If supervisors are not trained to coach safety, respond well to reporting, and manage conflict fairly, your culture will vary wildly by department.

Investing in supervisor development is culture work.

Case Examples: How SC³ Shows Up in Real Life

Public agency parks operations

A parks division has frequent strains and sprains. Supervisors believe injuries are "just part of field work." Near misses are rarely documented. When a serious injury occurs, leadership demands more forms, but staffing and equipment do not change. That is classic blindness drifting toward pre-competence once leaders start listening to crews and invest in carts, lifting aids, and realistic job planning.

Healthcare unit under staffing strain

A hospital unit is seeing an increase in patient-handling injuries and conflict incidents. Staff report "we don't have time" as the main barrier. Leadership wants training, but the real fix includes staffing, lift equipment access, and a better escalation pathway for behavioral risk. That is incapacity moving toward competence when leaders align resources with expectations.

School district maintenance and facilities

A district has a solid safety manual, but contractors and internal staff have different standards, and hazardous tasks get done "the way the old guys taught me." After a near miss, leadership creates a small standard toolkit: JHAs for high-risk tasks, consistent lockout tagging practices, and supervisor walk-throughs that are coaching-based, not disciplinary. That is pre-competence moving into competence.

A Practical SC³ Roadmap: What to Do in the Next 90 Days

If you want this chapter to turn into action, start here.

First 30 days

- Identify the top 3 repeat loss drivers by department and cause.

- Do leadership walk-throughs focused on barriers and constraints, not "gotcha."

- Audit your corrective action closure rate and remove bottlenecks.

Days 31–60

- Run a short pulse check (or listening sessions) focused on speak-up, follow-through, and supervisor consistency.

- Pick 2 visible fixes that frontline staff have asked for repeatedly, and complete them fast.

- Train supervisors on responding to reporting without blame and with clear next steps.

Days 61–90

- Standardize one high-risk process (example: vehicle backing, ladder use, lockout/tagout, patient handling, after-hours callouts).

- Add 3–5 leading indicators to your leadership dashboard that reflect culture, not just compliance.

- Hold a learning review on one incident or near miss using barrier thinking, then share the lessons and the fix.

The theme is simple: credibility grows when people see action.

Conclusion: Culture Is Your Most Powerful Control

Risk programs do not fail because people do not know the rules. They fail because the real operating system of the workplace rewards speed over care, silence over truth, and blame over learning.

The SC^3 continuum gives you a way to name your reality without sugarcoating it. Once you can name it, you can change it. When culture improves, it shows up everywhere: fewer repeat injuries, faster reporting, stronger follow-through, better morale, and more stable costs.

In the next chapter, we move from culture as the "human core" to the practical machinery of engaging and developing the workforce through training and engagement, where culture either becomes real or remains a slogan.

References

Dekker, S. (2014). *Just culture: Balancing safety and accountability* (2nd ed.). Ashgate.

Edmondson, A. (1999). Psychological safety and learning behavior in work teams. *Administrative Science Quarterly, 44*(2), 350–383.

Guldenmund, F. W. (2000). The nature of safety culture: A review of theory and research. *Safety Science, 34*(1–3), 215–257.

Hollnagel, E. (2014). *Safety-I and Safety-II: The past and future of safety management.* Ashgate.

Reason, J. (1997). *Managing the risks of organizational accidents.* Ashgate.

Schein, E. H. (2010). *Organizational culture and leadership* (4th ed.). Jossey-Bass.

Zohar, D. (1980). Safety climate in industrial organizations: Theoretical and applied implications. *Journal of Applied Psychology, 65*(1), 96–102.

Chapter 5
Safety Training and Workforce Engagement

Making Learning Stick for Field Staff, Supervisors, and Leaders

Making Learning Stick for Field Staff, Supervisors, and Leaders

Safety training has a branding problem. In too many organizations, "training" is what happens after someone gets hurt, after a regulator shows up, or after leadership gets nervous. People can feel that. They walk into the room already knowing the goal is coverage, not growth. Then we act surprised when nothing changes, or worse, when people start treating safety as paperwork they have to survive. If you want cost control and safety excellence, training cannot be a punishment, a checkbox, or a yearly lecture that disappears the moment the shift starts. It has to feel useful, grounded in real work, and supported by the environment people return to.

At its best, training does something simple and powerful. It changes what people notice, how they talk to each other, and what they choose to do when the easy option is also the risky option. That is why training is not separate from culture. It is one of the main ways culture is taught and reinforced.

The core idea of this chapter is straightforward: adults learn differently from kids, different roles need different training, and learning does not "transfer" into behavior unless the workplace makes it practical and expected. When training is designed with those truths in mind and tied to the loss drivers you actually have, it becomes one of the most reliable levers you can pull for both culture and cost.

What Adults Actually Learn From at Work

Most safety training fails for predictable reasons. It is too generic, too long, and too disconnected from the decisions people make in real time. Adults do not learn best when they are treated as empty containers. They learn best when the content solves a problem they recognize, respects the experience they already carry, and lets them apply something immediately.

Think about a maintenance crew, a school custodian, a park worker, or a nurse. They are not short on information. They are short on time, tools, staffing, and patience for training that ignores the reality of their job. When training starts with "Here are the definitions," you lose them. When it starts with "Here is what is happening in our work and here's what we can do differently tomorrow," you have a chance.

That "why" matters more than most leaders think. You can feel the room change when training opens with a real story from your organization or a pattern from your own claims data. People may not love it, but they recognize it. Relevance is the first form of respect.

Adult learning also hinges on participation. People need to talk through real situations, compare how they handle the work, and pressure test what "safe" looks like when constraints show up. Training that makes room for that conversation isn't softer. It's stronger, because it surfaces the real barriers instead of pretending they do not exist.

Engagement Beats Lecture

There's a reason scenario-based and hands-on methods consistently outperform lecture-only formats in changing safety behavior. People remember what they practice, not what they are told once while multitasking. You can deliver the best presentation in the world, but if participants do not rehearse the decision points, the muscle memory never forms.

High-engagement safety training usually has a few consistent features. It uses situations people recognize. It focuses on decisions, not just rules. It creates short moments where people have to choose an action, explain it, and hear how others would handle it. It gives feedback without humiliation. And it keeps returning to the question that drives outcomes: what will you do when the "right way" conflicts with speed, convenience, or habit?

Here is a practical example. A city has recurring back strains in parks and public works. A traditional response is a yearly lifting class. A stronger response is a short module built around the actual tasks that are driving the claims: loading bags, moving cans, lifting equipment, handling awkward objects, and working at odd heights. The training becomes less about anatomy and more about decisions and setup. Where do you stage materials? What do you do when you do not have the right cart? When do you ask for a second person? What does a good supervisor's response look like when a worker says, "This setup isn't safe"?

When training is built that way, you stop "teaching safety" in the abstract and start teaching people how to run their job with fewer losses.

Transfer Is the Real Battle

Even well-designed training can fail if the workplace punishes the behaviors you are trying to build. This is the "transfer problem." People can nod along in class, even mean it, then return to a jobsite where the supervisor rewards speed, the equipment is missing, the staffing is thin, and nobody wants to hear about delays. In that environment, the safe way becomes the slow way. Over time, the safe way becomes optional.

Transfer improves when the environment reinforces learning in simple, visible ways. Supervisors ask about it. Leaders notice it. Tools and equipment support it. Time is built into the job planning for doing it correctly. And when someone speaks up, the response is not ridicule or eye-rolling.

A lot of organizations unintentionally sabotage transfer by treating training as the fix. Training is only one part of the fix. If the hazard is structural, and the only "control" is a classroom reminder, the system will win. People will drift back to the path of least resistance.

So the right question for leadership is not, "Did they attend training?" It's, "Did the conditions they returned to allow the training to be used?"

Core Design Principles That Make Training Stick

Safety training that changes behavior tends to follow a few design principles. You do not need a complex learning department to apply them. You need discipline and focus.

Start with the actual loss drivers. Build training around what is happening in your organization, not what a generic catalog says you should cover. If your top drivers are vehicle incidents, strains, slips, and conflict exposure, your training calendar should reflect that reality.

Keep it short and frequent. People learn better in smaller segments repeated over time than in one long annual event. This is especially true for frontline staff who are physically tired and operating under time pressure.

Use practice, not just explanation. You can keep some classroom content, but the center of gravity should be scenarios, walk-throughs, demonstrations, and conversations anchored in real work.

Make the "safe way" concrete. If the training ends with "be careful," it will not change anything. People need to know what to do, what to check, what to say, and what "good" looks like in a real moment.

Close the loop. When training reveals barriers, the organization must address at least some of them. Nothing kills engagement faster than asking workers to identify hazards and then doing nothing with what they told you.

Different Audiences Need Different Training

One of the most common mistakes is delivering the same training to everyone and calling it "consistent." Consistency does not mean identical. It means aligned.

Field staff: practical, relevant, and respectful of experience

Frontline staff need training that looks like their job. It should use their language, their tools, their constraints. It should focus on hazards that show up in their day, not theoretical risks. They should leave with one or two clear behaviors they can actually apply in the next shift.

It also helps to acknowledge something leaders often ignore: many frontline workers have already learned how to stay safe in imperfect conditions. Good training treats that experience as an asset. It draws it out, validates what is effective, and challenges what is risky in a way that does not insult people.

Supervisors: from message carrier to coach

Supervisors are the hinge between policy and practice. If you train everyone except supervisors, you are building a house with no beams. Supervisors need a different kind of training. They need to know how to coach behavior in the moment, how to respond to reporting without blame, and how to create accountability that is fair and consistent.

Supervisor training should sound like real life. How do you address repeated shortcuts without escalating conflict? What do you do when a worker says, "We don't have the equipment for that"? How do you run a short safety conversation at the start of a shift that doesn't feel like a lecture? How do you use basic data to spot patterns without turning it into a gotcha game?

If you can build supervisors' confidence in those skills, transfer improves because safety becomes part of daily management rather than a yearly event.

Executives and senior leaders: strategic, short, and tied to outcomes

Executives do not need detailed technical modules on every hazard. They need clarity on what is driving cost, what the risk trends are telling them, and how leadership decisions either strengthen or weaken safety. Their training should link directly to outcomes they already care about: total cost of risk, service reliability, staffing strain, turnover, and public trust.

For leaders, it often works best to structure training around case examples and decisions. What do we fund, what do we defer, what do we tolerate, and what do we treat as non-negotiable? That approach also makes it clear that safety culture is not "owned" by the safety team. It is owned by leadership choices.

Blending Methods Without Creating Noise

Most organizations need a mix of training methods. A learning management system can be useful for consistency and documentation, but it should not be treated as the main engine of behavior change. Toolbox talks can work, but only if they are not read from a script in two minutes while everyone waits to start work. Peer learning can be powerful, especially when experienced employees are trained to model and coach safer practices.

The best blend usually looks like this: short foundational content for consistency, paired with recurring on-the-job conversations and periodic hands-on refreshers focused on high-risk tasks. The goal is not to build a giant library. The goal is to build repetition around the few behaviors that will actually change your outcomes.

If you want a quick test of whether your training mix is working, ask frontline staff a simple question: "What have you changed because of training in the last 60 days?" If they cannot answer, you have an activity problem, not a learning system.

Measuring Training Effectiveness Without Overcomplicating It

Training measurements often get stuck in extremes. Some organizations measure nothing beyond attendance. Others try to build a graduate-level evaluation program that nobody has time to maintain.

You can do something practical without pretending that training is easy to measure.

Start with basic feedback, but do not confuse "people liked it" with "it changed anything." Then look for behavior signals. Are supervisors actually having the safety conversations they were trained to have? Are near misses being reported more, and are they of better quality? Are corrective actions being closed more consistently? Are the same job tasks still driving the same injury patterns?

Finally, tie training to risk metrics you already track. If vehicle incidents are a top driver, measure whether the behaviors taught are showing up in practice, then watch the trend line over time. If your top workers' comp driver is strains, track whether targeted task training correlates with fewer claims, fewer repeat injuries, and faster return to work. The time lag matters, so leaders need to understand they are watching trend shifts, not instant results.

If you keep measurement grounded and consistent, you build credibility. Training stops being a cost center and becomes a visible investment with trackable outcomes.

Training as Engagement, Not Punishment

One of the most important shifts an organization can make is how it frames training after an incident. If training is always the consequence, it will be resented. People will attend, sign, and mentally check out. If training is framed as support and improvement, it becomes something people can participate in without shame.

That does not mean avoiding accountability. It means being clear about what training is for. Training is for capability building and behavior reinforcement. Accountability is for choices and standards. When those two are blurred, you end up with a culture where people hide problems because they do not want the response that comes with admitting one.

A healthier approach is to treat training as part of a learning loop. Something happens, you review it, identify where people need better tools, more precise guidance, or better coaching, and you adjust the system. People are far more willing to engage when they see that the organization is willing to learn too.

Closing

Safety training is often treated like a requirement. In high-performing organizations, it is treated like a leadership tool. Done well, it builds shared language, sharpens judgment, strengthens supervisor coaching, and reinforces the cultural expectation that safety is not optional. Done poorly, it becomes background noise that people learn to tolerate.

If you want training to improve both culture and cost, focus on relevance, practice, and transfer. Train different roles differently, but keep them aligned. Measure what matters, not just what is easy to count. Then make sure the environment people return to supports what you taught. When those pieces come together, training stops being something you "deliver" and becomes something the organization uses to run work better.

References

Baldwin, T. T., & Ford, J. K. (1988). Transfer of training: A review and directions for future research. *Personnel Psychology, 41*(1), 63–105.

Bęś, P., & Strzałkowski, P. (2024). Analysis of the effectiveness of safety training methods. *Sustainability, 16*(7), 2732.

Burke, M. J., Sarpy, S. A., Smith-Crowe, K., Chan-Serafin, S., Salvador, R. O., & Islam, G. (2006). Relative effectiveness of worker safety and health training methods. *American Journal of Public Health, 96*(2), 315–324.

Hughes, A. M., Zajac, S., Woods, A. L., & Salas, E. (2020). The role of work environment in training transfer. *Human Resource Development Review, 19*(1), 17–43.

Kirkpatrick, J. D., & Kirkpatrick, W. K. (2016). *Kirkpatrick's four levels of training evaluation.* ATD Press.

Knapke, J. M., Spector, J. M., & Baker, M. (2024). Adult learning principles in workplace training: A practical review. *Journal of Workplace Learning, 36*(2), 123–140.

Ramachandran, G. (2023). Safety training and organizational outcomes: Linking learning to performance. *Safety Science, 164*, 106174.

Rouse, W. B. (2011). *Design for success: A human-centered approach to training and performance.* Wiley.

Salas, E., DiazGranados, D., Klein, C., Burke, C. S., Stagl, K. C., Goodwin, G. F., & Halpin, S. M. (2008). Does team training improve team performance? A meta-analysis. *Human Factors, 50*(6), 903–933.

Chapter 6
Meetings Matter

Elevating Risk Conversations Through Thoughtful
Engagement

Elevating Risk Conversations Through Thoughtful Engagement

The funny thing about risk conversations is that everyone agrees they're important right up until the calendar invite hits. Then it becomes one more hour wedged between emergencies, email, and whatever operational fire is burning the hottest that day. Over time, that pattern trains the organization to treat risk like a side topic instead of a condition of performance. Not because people do not care, but because the meeting itself is not built to carry the weight it is supposed to carry.

In most organizations, meetings are where risk either gets managed or quietly multiplied. A well-run meeting surfaces weak signals, forces tradeoffs into the open, assigns ownership, and creates follow-through. A poorly run meeting does the opposite. It replaces decisions with discussion, hides discomfort behind "updates," and sends people back to work with the same confusion they walked in with. If you want a more resilient organization, you do not start with a new dashboard. You start with better conversations, and meetings are the most controllable place to practice them (Rogelberg, 2019; Mroz & Allen, 2018).

Meetings are not neutral. They either reduce uncertainty or spread it, depending on how they are designed and led. A risk leader's credibility is often built in the meeting room, not in the policy manual, because that is where priorities get tested in real time. The quality of meetings shapes psychological safety, and psychological safety shapes whether people share early warning signs or stay quiet until a problem becomes expensive (Edmondson, 1999; Westrum, 2004). Finally, consistent follow-through is what turns "risk talk" into risk control, and the meeting is the most direct mechanism most leaders have to create that discipline (COSO, 2017; ISO, 2018).

The Meeting as a Risk Control, Not a Calendar Habit

Risk management is full of tools, registers, inspections, analytics, audits. All of them matter. But if leaders do not have a predictable forum where risk gets discussed with clarity, urgency, and accountability, the tools become performative. They may look impressive in a binder, yet the organization keeps repeating the same incidents, the same near misses, and the same late-stage surprises.

ISO 31000 places communication and consultation as a continuous element of risk management, not a side task (ISO, 2018). COSO emphasizes information, communication, and reporting as part of a functioning enterprise risk system, not simply a reporting layer after decisions are made (COSO, 2017). That is the core idea: risk is managed through decisions, and decisions are usually made, shaped, delayed, or avoided in meetings.

When meetings are treated as "status updates," risk becomes something that happens to the organization. When meetings are treated as decision forums, risk becomes something the organization actively governs.

Purpose Before Agenda: What This Meeting Is For

Most risk meetings fail for a simple reason. They are scheduled before anyone decides what the meeting is supposed to produce. An agenda is not a list of topics. It is a sequence of decisions. That is why the first question is not "What should we cover?" The first question is "What must be true when we leave?"

A risk meeting should typically produce one or more of the following outcomes:

A decision, such as approving a control, selecting a vendor, accepting a risk, or changing a process. An alignment, such as agreeing on a message before it moves upward to executive leadership or outward to employees. A commitment, such as assigning owners, deadlines, and resources to close a gap. Or a learning, such as capturing what happened in an incident or near miss, and agreeing on what will change.

Steven Rogelberg's meeting research is blunt on this point. Meetings are more effective when they are designed around outcomes and when participants understand why they are there (Rogelberg, 2019). People tolerate time when they can see the purpose. They resent the time when the purpose is vague.

If you are leading the meeting, say the purpose plainly in the first minute. If you are attending the meeting, ask for the purpose before you accept the invite. Over time, that one move raises the organization's standard for what earns people's time.

The "Meeting Before the Meeting" and the Discipline of Alignment

Some risk conversations cannot succeed cold. If you walk into a room where key stakeholders are already dug in, you are not facilitating. You are refereeing. That is where the meeting before the meeting becomes a legitimate leadership tool.

This is not about backroom deals. It is about preventing public confusion. If the risk manager and the operational leader are not aligned on the real question being asked, the meeting will drift, and the group will spend its time watching two leaders negotiate in real time. That usually produces one of two outcomes: either the group disengages, or the group splits into camps.

A short pre-meeting conversation can clarify what is truly on the table, what information is missing, what constraints are real, and what decision criteria will be used. Done correctly, it makes the real meeting more honest, not less. It reduces the temptation for performative positions and increases the chance that disagreements become productive.

This matters even more in public-sector environments, school districts, and agencies where risk decisions are tied to labor relations, public scrutiny, and political pressure. In those settings, ambiguity becomes fuel for mistrust. Alignment does not eliminate disagreement. It makes disagreement manageable.

Building an Agenda That Can Hold a Real Risk Conversation

A risk-focused agenda should have rhythm. If everything is urgent, nothing is. If everything is discussed, nothing is decided.

A practical structure looks like this:

Start with a short risk snapshot. What changed since last time? New incidents, claims trends, new regulatory requirements, emerging operational hazards, vendor issues, and community complaints. The goal is not storytelling. It is situational awareness.

Then move into decision items. The meeting should prioritize what needs a decision now, not what is easiest to talk about. When organizations do not decide, they drift, and drift is a hidden risk multiplier.

After making decisions, allocate time for learning. This is where near misses, incidents, or operational surprises get reviewed without blame, with a focus on what failed in the system and what will change in practice (Reason, 1997; Dekker, 2012).

Close with commitments. Who is doing what, by when, and what support do they need? The meeting ends when ownership is clear.

This structure also helps with meeting fatigue. Research on meeting recovery and virtual meeting fatigue suggests that meeting quality matters and that poor meetings drain attention, requiring recovery time before people can return to productive work (Allen et al., 2022). A meeting that wanders is not just annoying. It is a productivity tax that repeats all day.

Psychological Safety: The Hidden Infrastructure of Risk Reporting

You can have the best agenda in the world and still miss the real risks if people do not feel safe enough to speak honestly. Amy Edmondson's work on psychological safety shows that teams learn and improve when people believe they can speak up, ask questions, and admit mistakes without fear of humiliation or punishment (Edmondson, 1999). In risk management, that is not a "culture nice-to-have." It is the difference between early warning and late catastrophe.

Ron Westrum's typology of organizational cultures also highlights how information flow predicts safety performance. Organizations that punish messengers, hoard information, or discourage dissent create conditions where weak signals die quietly (Westrum, 2004). That is how small operational issues become major incidents.

Meetings are where psychological safety becomes visible. Watch for these signals:

People avoid naming uncertainty. Concerns get softened into vague language. Questions become private side conversations after the meeting. The same person always speaks while others stay silent. Disagreement feels personal instead of analytical.

A risk leader's job is to change those dynamics without turning the meeting into group therapy. The move is simple and powerful: normalize candor. Ask better questions. Reward early reporting. Separate blame from accountability.

Just culture thinking helps here. The goal is not to remove accountability. The goal is to apply it fairly, in a way that encourages learning rather than concealment (Dekker, 2012). A meeting culture that only punishes outcomes will always be late to risk. A meeting culture that examines systems will get earlier signals.

Lateness, Attention, and Respect: Small Behaviors That Predict Big Outcomes

In many organizations, lateness is treated as normal. People drift in, half listening, juggling email, apologizing with a quick joke. That feels minor until you recognize what it actually signals: "This time does not matter." When that becomes normal, the meeting becomes a weak governance mechanism.

Research has examined meeting lateness and its consequences, and it is not harmless. Lateness affects meeting processes and outcomes by disrupting attention, reducing shared context, and signaling low commitment (Allen et al., 2018). In risk work, those disruptions matter because decisions often hinge on details that do not repeat themselves later.

The standard does not have to be rigid. It does have to be consistent. Start on time. End on time. If you need five minutes to settle in, build it into the schedule, but do not pretend it is optional. Meeting discipline is not about control. It is about respect for the work.

Turning Incidents Into Learning Instead of Blame

A common risk meeting failure is the post-incident discussion that goes nowhere. Everyone nods, everyone agrees it should not happen again, and nothing changes. That is how organizations accumulate "lessons learned" with no learning.

James Reason's work on organizational accidents argues that major failures rarely come from a single bad choice. They come from layers of small conditions that line up, often invisible until after the event (Reason, 1997). That is why the incident discussion must focus on system conditions: staffing, training, supervision, equipment design, workload, conflicting priorities, unclear procedures, and normalization of deviance.

A productive incident review in a meeting does a few specific things:

It clarifies what happened, using facts and timeline rather than opinions. It identifies contributing factors across people, process, environment, and leadership. It decides what controls will change, who owns them, and how effectiveness will be measured. And it circles back later to confirm the change actually took hold.

That last part is where most organizations fail. They treat incident review as a one-time conversation. Risk management treats it as a loop.

The Follow-Through Gap: Where Good Meetings Go to Die

A meeting can feel productive and still be useless. The difference is follow-through.

A practical risk leader treats action items like controls. If a control is not implemented, monitored, and sustained, it is not real. Meeting commitments are the same. If tasks get assigned without deadlines, resources, and a check-back point, they become polite wishes.

This is where governance frameworks and meeting discipline meet. COSO emphasizes oversight and accountability, not just risk identification (COSO, 2017). ISO emphasizes monitoring and review, not just analysis (ISO, 2018). If meeting outcomes are not tracked, the meeting becomes a talk loop.

A simple approach is to treat the first five minutes of every risk meeting as a closure loop. What did we commit to last time? What is done? What is stuck? What help is needed? Over time, that pattern changes the organization. People stop volunteering vague tasks because they know they will be asked about them. That is not pressure. That is maturity.

Meeting Overload and the Myth of "More Coordination"

Many organizations respond to complexity by adding meetings. It feels logical. More coordination should reduce risk. In practice, meeting overload can create new risks by destroying focus, delaying decisions, and burning out key staff.

Harvard Business Review has noted how meeting time has increased dramatically over the decades, with executives spending significant hours per week in meetings, often at the expense of real work (Perlow et al., 2017). The psychological experience of meeting overload is also well documented in organizational commentary and research-informed analysis: too many meetings can reduce engagement, increase stress, and degrade performance (Perlow et al., 2017; Mroz & Allen, 2018).

The risk lens here is straightforward. If your best people cannot do deep work, you get shallow controls. You get templates instead of tailored solutions. You get "check the box" compliance. You get rushed training. You get deferred maintenance. Those are not soft problems. They are precursors to incidents and claims.

This is where leadership has to be honest. Some meetings exist because leaders do not trust delegation. Some exist because decisions are avoided. Some exist because communication channels are weak, so meetings become the default. If you want fewer meetings, you usually need clearer decision rights and better written communication, not just better facilitation.

Virtual and Hybrid Meetings: Making Risk Conversations Work on a Screen

Virtual meetings did not create bad meetings, but they magnified their cost. When a virtual meeting is unclear, people multitask. When it is boring, people disappear behind muted cameras. When it is tense, people disengage silently. Meeting fatigue is real, and research suggests recovery time and meeting quality matter for how drained people feel afterward (Allen et al., 2022).

For risk meetings, virtual does not have to mean weaker. It just requires a stronger structure. State the purpose clearly. Use the agenda as a decision path, not a topic list. Call on people intentionally, especially quieter operational voices who may have the most valuable weak-signal information. Use short pauses for questions so people can actually jump in. Close with explicit ownership and next steps.

Hybrid meetings, where some people are in a room, and others are remote, require extra care. Remote participants are the first to be ignored and the last to speak. If the meeting is about risk, that is dangerous. You can fix it with small habits: assign a facilitator to watch the chat, prioritize remote voices early, and avoid side conversations in the room.

What This Looks Like in the Real World

In a city environment, a risk meeting might involve Public Works, Parks, Fleet, HR, and Finance. Each group has its own pressures. Parks wants events to go smoothly. Fleet wants vehicles back on the road. HR wants consistent policy. Finance wants stability. Risk wants controls that prevent repeat loss. If the meeting is not designed for decisions, it becomes a polite tour of competing priorities.

A well-run version of that meeting makes tradeoffs visible. If staffing shortages are driving rushed work, the meeting forces a decision: reduce scope, adjust schedules, bring in temporary support, or accept higher risk knowingly. That is governance. It is not comfortable, but it is honest.

In a school district, the risk meeting might involve Maintenance and Operations, Safety, HR, and site leadership. The risks include not just injuries and claims, but community trust and student safety. Psychological safety matters here because frontline employees often see the hazards first: broken gates, poor lighting, unsecured equipment, escalating behaviors, and rushed repairs. If those voices do not speak, the system stays blind until something goes wrong (Edmondson, 1999; Westrum, 2004).

In healthcare, a risk meeting might involve nursing leadership, facilities, compliance, and security. The stakes are obvious. The meeting must support a just culture in which incident reporting leads to system improvements, not to fear and silence (Dekker, 2012; Reason, 1997). When that happens, near misses become gifts. When it does not, near misses become rehearsals for harm.

Different settings, same principle. Meetings either carry risk intelligence upward or bury it under "updates."

Closing

A risk leader does not need to be the loudest person in the room. They need to be the person who protects the quality of the conversation. That means being disciplined about purpose, insisting on decisions, and refusing to let commitments dissolve into ambiguity. It also means shaping a meeting culture where people can name problems early without fear, because early truth is always cheaper than late truth (Edmondson, 1999; Westrum, 2004).

If you want a simple standard to hold yourself to, try this: every risk meeting should end with at least one clear decision, one clear commitment, and one clear learning. If it does not, ask why it existed. Then change it. Over time, you will notice something important. Your risk program will feel less like a department and more like a leadership function, because your meetings will start doing what they were always supposed to do: turning uncertainty into action.

References

Allen, J. A., Lehmann-Willenbrock, N., & Rogelberg, S. G. (2018). Let's get this meeting started: Meeting lateness and actual meeting outcomes. *Journal of Organizational Behavior*.

Allen, J. A., Reiter-Palmon, R., Crowe, J., & Scott, C. (2022). Why am I so exhausted? Exploring meeting-to-work transition time and recovery from virtual meeting fatigue. *PLOS ONE, 17*(8), e0272456.

Committee of Sponsoring Organizations of the Treadway Commission. (2017). *Enterprise risk management: Integrating with strategy and performance.*

Dekker, S. (2012). *Just culture: Balancing safety and accountability* (2nd ed.). Ashgate.

Edmondson, A. C. (1999). Psychological safety and learning behavior in work teams. *Administrative Science Quarterly, 44*(2), 350–383.

International Organization for Standardization. (2018). *ISO 31000:2018 Risk management—Guidelines*. ISO.

Mroz, J. E., & Allen, J. A. (2018). Do we really need another meeting? The science of workplace meetings. *Current Directions in Psychological Science.*

Perlow, L. A., Hadley, C. N., & Eun, E. (2017, July–August). Stop the meeting madness. *Harvard Business Review.*

Reason, J. (1997). *Managing the risks of organizational accidents*. Ashgate.

Rogelberg, S. G. (2019). *The surprising science of meetings: How you can lead your team to peak performance*. Oxford University Press.

Westrum, R. (2004). A typology of organizational cultures. *Quality & Safety in Health Care, 13*(Suppl 2), ii22–ii27.

Chapter 7
Destroyers of a Safety Culture in Organizations

How Small Leadership Signals Quietly Undermine Trust, Reporting, and Prevention

Destroyers of a Safety Culture in Organizations

Most organizations do not wake up one day and decide to be unsafe. What happens is slower and more ordinary than that. A shortcut becomes normal because the job still got done. A near miss gets laughed off because nobody got hurt. A supervisor stops reporting hazards because the last three reports went nowhere. A manager learns that the fastest way to keep the peace is to avoid hard conversations. Then a serious injury hits, and everyone suddenly "can't believe it happened."

A safety culture does not collapse from one bad leader or one broken policy. It erodes when everyday signals tell people that safety is optional, that speaking up is risky, or that the organization values the appearance of control more than the reality of it. That erosion shows up in patterns you can actually see and measure: underreporting, repeated incidents of the same type, maintenance backlog, inconsistent enforcement, and a widening gap between what leaders say and what workers experience (Zohar, 1980; Reason, 1997).

Safety culture gets destroyed when production and image consistently win the tie, even in small moments, because employees learn what the organization truly rewards. Blame and fear shut down reporting, and without reporting, leaders lose the early warning signs that prevent serious harm (Edmondson, 1999; Westrum, 2004). Drift is real: once deviance becomes routine, people stop noticing it, and risk becomes invisible until it becomes catastrophic (Vaughan, 1996; Reason, 1997). The organizations that protect safety over time build reliable feedback loops, visible follow-through, and clear accountability, not just training and slogans (OSHA, 2016; ISO, 2018).

When "Getting It Done" Beats "Doing It Right"

Every safety culture has a scoreboard, even if it is never written down. People look at what gets praised, promoted, and protected. They also notice what gets tolerated.

When schedule pressure is treated like a permanent emergency, safety becomes negotiable. In meetings, it sounds like, "We'll fix it later," "Just this once," or "We don't have time for all that." In the field, it becomes rushed setups, skipped steps, incomplete barricades, and equipment that should be tagged out but "still works." The hard part is that those choices often come from good intentions. People want to serve the public. They want to keep services running. They do not want to be the reason work slows down.

But repeated tradeoffs teach the workforce something dangerous: safety is what you do when things are calm, not what you do when things are real. That is backwards. High-reliability organizations do not treat safety as a "nice weather" practice. They build habits for operating under stress, which is why they emphasize attentiveness to weak signals and a preoccupation with small failures before they become big ones (Weick & Sutcliffe, 2007).

Here is what this destroyer looks like in real life:

- A supervisor quietly encourages crews to "be efficient" but only calls out safety when something goes wrong.

- Staffing shortages become a permanent excuse, instead of a risk factor that requires a decision, a scope change, or added controls.

- Unsafe conditions are treated as "part of the job," especially in maintenance, parks, custodial, transportation, healthcare, and public-facing roles.

The fix is not motivational posters. It is leadership honesty. If your workload exceeds your capacity to do it safely, you have a risk decision to make. Leaders have to either adjust scope, add staffing, change methods, or accept risk explicitly and ethically. Pretending you can do more with less forever is not "toughness." It is denial.

Leadership Inconsistency and the Credibility Gap

If you want to destroy a safety culture quickly, say "Safety is our top priority" and then behave as if it is not. The workforce hears that as manipulation, not inspiration.

Safety culture is built on perceived priorities. Zohar's early safety climate work showed that employees' perceptions of how much leaders truly value safety predict safety-related behavior (Zohar, 1980). In plain terms, people do what they believe management really wants, not what the mission statement says.

The credibility gap shows up in small contradictions:

- Leaders talk about safety but never attend safety meetings.

- Leaders ask for reports but never respond to the issues raised.

- Leaders enforce rules strictly after an incident, then loosen enforcement when pressure rises.

- Leaders punish a person for reporting a hazard because "it makes us look bad."

Even well-meaning leaders accidentally create this gap. They walk a site visit and praise productivity, then later wonder why shortcuts are common. They demand "no surprises," and then are surprised nobody tells them bad news early. The message becomes: do not bring problems, bring solutions, and do not bring problems that cost money.

A strong safety culture requires visible, consistent leadership behaviors. OSHA's recommended practices emphasize management leadership and worker participation as core elements of effective safety and health programs (OSHA, 2016). That means leaders do not just approve policies. They model priorities, allocate resources, and respond in ways that make reporting and improvement worthwhile.

Blame Culture, Fear, and the Collapse of Reporting

Most organizations claim they want transparency. Then they create consequences for transparency.

Blame culture is one of the most reliable destroyers of safety culture because it shuts down the most valuable asset you have: information. When people believe that reporting leads to punishment, humiliation, or career damage, they stop reporting. They might still talk privately, but the organization's formal channels go quiet. Leaders interpret the silence as "things are improving," when in reality visibility is declining.

Psychological safety is the condition that allows people to share concerns, admit mistakes, and ask questions without fear of embarrassment or retaliation (Edmondson, 1999). In safety work, psychological safety is not soft. It is what keeps weak signals alive long enough to be acted on.

Westrum's work on organizational culture emphasizes information flow. In healthy cultures, messengers are not punished, and problems are surfaced early. In pathological cultures, information is hoarded, and bad news is suppressed (Westrum, 2004).

You can spot a blame-driven safety culture by the language people use:

- "Don't write that down."

- "That'll get someone in trouble."

- "Just handle it."

- "They'll make a big deal out of it."

When those phrases become normal, your incident rates might look good on paper, but your real risk is rising.

A just culture approach helps organizations separate human error, at-risk behavior, and reckless behavior, and respond in ways that improve systems while preserving accountability (Dekker, 2012). The point is not to remove responsibility. The point is to stop using blame as a substitute for learning.

Normalization of Deviance and Slow Drift Into Danger

Some of the most serious failures in history did not happen because people ignored rules. They happened because people followed routine, and the routine had quietly become unsafe.

Diane Vaughan's concept of normalization of deviance describes how organizations gradually accept rule-bending and anomalies as normal, especially in complex, high-pressure environments (Vaughan, 1996). Over time, the abnormal becomes ordinary. The danger stops feeling like danger.

Reason's work on organizational accidents helps explain why this drift is so hard to see in real time. Major accidents are rarely the result of one cause. They are the result of layered defenses weakening while work continues to "succeed" until it suddenly does not (Reason, 1997).

In everyday workplaces, normalization of deviance looks like:

- PPE exceptions that become the real standard.
- Lockout-tagout steps that get skipped because "it's just a quick fix."
- Incomplete inspections that still get signed off.
- Temporary repairs that become permanent.
- Near misses that are treated as proof of skill instead of proof of vulnerability.

The most dangerous part is that drift is reinforced by success. If nothing bad happened, the workaround is seen as validated. That is why leaders have to treat small deviations as data, not as proof that "we're fine." High-reliability thinking pushes organizations to treat near misses and anomalies as gifts because they reveal where the system is fragile (Weick & Sutcliffe, 2007).

Safety Metrics That Mislead and Management That Looks Away

A safety culture is not destroyed only by bad behavior. It is also destroyed by bad measurement.

If leaders rely primarily on lagging indicators such as injury rates and claims costs, they often miss the real story until it is too late. Lagging metrics tell you what happened. They do not tell you what is about to happen. They also create incentives to hide problems, especially when the organization ties recognition or discipline to "good numbers."

Good measurement does not mean more data. It means better signals.

Leading indicators can be imperfect, too, but they push the organization toward prevention: hazard reports, near-miss reporting, corrective action closure rates, safety observation quality, training competency checks, maintenance completion rates, and supervisor field contact frequency. In other words, measures of whether controls are alive.

OSHA's recommended practices emphasize hazard identification, prevention and control, training, and program evaluation as core program elements (OSHA, 2016). Those elements are measurable and harder to fake than an injury rate.

The destroyer is when leadership uses metrics as a shield instead of a flashlight. "Our incident rate is low" becomes an excuse to stop asking hard questions. Meanwhile, near-miss reporting drops, maintenance backlogs rise, and staff complaints increase. The organization is not safer. It is quieter.

Training as Theater and the Myth of "We Covered It"

Most safety failures are not caused by people lacking information. They are caused by people working in conditions where safe work is harder than unsafe work.

Training matters, but training alone cannot carry a safety culture. ISO 45001 emphasizes competence, worker participation, and continual improvement within a management system, not just training events (ISO, 2018). When organizations treat training as the primary control, they often avoid harder work: redesigning tasks, improving equipment, clarifying procedures, and addressing staffing and supervision.

Training becomes theater when:

- It is generic and disconnected from actual hazards.

- It happens after incidents, mainly to create documentation.

- It focuses on rules but not on real-world constraints.

- It does not include practice, observation, or coaching.

- It ends without verifying competence.

If you want to know whether training is helping, do not ask whether it was delivered. Ask whether the work changed. Ask whether supervisors can coach the behaviors. Ask whether the environment supports the behaviors. Ask whether hazard reports decreased because hazards were fixed, not because reporting collapsed.

Broken Follow-Through and Learned Helplessness

One of the fastest ways to destroy safety culture is to make reporting feel pointless.

If employees report hazards and nothing happens, they learn quickly. If corrective actions linger for months, they learn again. If the same problem comes up in every meeting and never closes, they stop bringing it up. That is not cynicism. It is adaptation.

This is where safety culture becomes a governance issue. Does the organization have a clear process for triaging hazards, assigning owners, funding fixes, and closing the loop back to the people who raised the concern? Does leadership review overdue corrective actions with the same seriousness as they review budget overruns?

OSHA's framework explicitly includes program evaluation and improvement, which implies that safety is a loop, not a one-time activity (OSHA, 2016). ISO 45001 similarly emphasizes improvement and management review (ISO, 2018). When that loop fails, people stop investing emotionally in the program. They do what they must to get through the day.

A practical sign of good culture is not "no hazards." It is fast, visible closure on hazards that matter, and honest communication about hazards that take longer to fix.

Fragmented Accountability, Contractors, and the "Not My Job" Trap

In modern organizations, work is often shared across internal teams, contractors, staffing agencies, vendors, and interdepartmental partners. That complexity creates a common destroyer: unclear responsibility.

When everyone touches the work, nobody owns the risk.

A safety culture gets weaker when:

- Contract language does not clearly define safety responsibilities and reporting expectations.

- Host employers assume contractors "handle their own safety" while contractors assume the host controls the site.

- Departments blame each other for hazards that live at the boundary, such as shared facilities, shared equipment, and shared workflows.

- Policies exist, but do not match how work is actually coordinated.

OSHA's recommended practices include communication and coordination for host employers, contractors, and staffing agencies for a reason. Handoffs and boundaries are where many serious failures occur (OSHA, 2016).

This is not solved by more paperwork. It is solved by clear expectations, joint walkthroughs, shared hazard-reporting pathways, and meeting structures in which cross-boundary issues are owned, tracked, and closed.

Closing

The organizations that protect safety culture over time are not perfect. They are honest. They treat small failures as valuable information. They reward reporting. They close loops. They measure what matters. They make hard decisions about workload and resources instead of pretending tradeoffs do not exist.

A safety culture is destroyed when the organization repeatedly teaches people that safety is optional, that speaking up is dangerous, or that nothing will change. Those lessons do not come from one big speech. They come from everyday behavior.

If you want to pressure-test your own culture, ask three simple questions and listen carefully to the answers: Do people report problems early? Do leaders respond consistently and fairly? Do fixes actually get implemented and sustained? If the answer is "sometimes," you have work to do. The good news is that culture is not mysterious. It is built from practices, and practices can be changed.

References

Committee of Sponsoring Organizations of the Treadway Commission. (2017). *Enterprise risk management: Integrating with strategy and performance.* COSO.

Dekker, S. (2012). *Just culture: Balancing safety and accountability* (2nd ed.). Ashgate.

Edmondson, A. C. (1999). Psychological safety and learning behavior in work teams. *Administrative Science Quarterly, 44*(4), 350–383.

International Organization for Standardization. (2018). *ISO 45001:2018 Occupational health and safety management systems: Requirements with guidance for use.* ISO.

Occupational Safety and Health Administration. (2016). *Recommended practices for safety and health programs.* U.S. Department of Labor.

Reason, J. (1997). *Managing the risks of organizational accidents.* Ashgate.

Vaughan, D. (1996). *The Challenger launch decision: Risky technology, culture, and deviance at NASA.* University of Chicago Press.

Weick, K. E., & Sutcliffe, K. M. (2007). *Managing the unexpected: Resilient performance in an age of uncertainty* (2nd ed.). Jossey-Bass.

Westrum, R. (2004). A typology of organizational cultures. *Quality & Safety in Health Care, 13*(Suppl 2), ii22–ii27.

Part III – Governance, Structure, and Leadership

Chapter 8
Reimagining Risk Management Governance

Who Should Risk Managers Report To?

Who Should Risk Managers Report To?

Ask ten organizations where the risk manager reports, and you will hear ten answers that all sound reasonable until something goes wrong. In one place, risk sits under Finance because claims dollars live there. In another, under HR, because workers' compensation and employee relations take up most of the day. In another, under Legal, because litigation is the loudest voice in the room. And in plenty of organizations, risk reports to Operations because that's "where the work happens."

Each structure has a logic. Each structure also has blind spots.

The governance question, "Who should risk managers report to?" is really about two competing needs that rarely live in perfect harmony. Risk needs independence, meaning the ability to say uncomfortable things without getting muted. Risk also needs influence, meaning enough proximity to decision-makers that concerns turn into decisions, resources, and behavior change. When you get the reporting line wrong, you either end up with a risk function that is "independent" but ignored, or "embedded" but captured.

Key learnings in this chapter are simple but not easy: the best reporting line is the one that protects risk's ability to speak honestly while keeping it close enough to the people who allocate resources and set priorities; reporting to a function that owns the outcome you are evaluating can create real conflicts, especially when cost, schedule, or reputation pressure rises; and the most durable governance models combine a clear primary reporting line with a formal dotted-line oversight path that reinforces independence, transparency, and escalation when needed (Committee of Sponsoring Organizations of the Treadway Commission [COSO], 2017; Institute of Internal Auditors [IIA], 2020; International Organization for Standardization [ISO], 2018; U.S. Government Accountability Office [GAO], 2025).

Why the Reporting Line Matters More Than People Think

Most risk professionals have lived some version of this: you see a pattern early, you raise it, and the response is polite but noncommittal. Then a preventable incident happens, or a claim explodes, and suddenly leadership wants to know why nobody flagged it. You did flag it. It just didn't travel with enough authority to change anything.

That is governance at work. Reporting lines determine what gets airtime, how fast issues escalate, and whether risk recommendations are treated as guidance or as "optional input." They also shape what risk teams feel safe to say. Even the strongest risk manager will start trimming their message if their reporting structure punishes candor.

COSO's ERM framework puts governance and culture front and center because governance is the scaffolding that makes risk management real, not theoretical (COSO, 2017). ISO 31000 similarly emphasizes leadership and integration. Risk management is not meant to be a separate discipline living off to the side. It is meant to be integrated into how the organization makes decisions (ISO, 2018). Those frameworks are not telling you where the risk manager "must" report. They are telling you that structure must support independence, integration, and consistent communication.

So the reporting question is not administrative. It is strategic.

The Core Tension: Independence Versus Influence

Risk functions often swing between two extremes.

On one extreme, risk is positioned so independently that it becomes advisory only. It can write reports and make recommendations, but it lacks the leverage to get traction. This happens when risk is isolated, under-resourced, or treated as a compliance function that appears mainly after incidents.

On the other extreme, risk is placed so close to one operational function that it gets captured by that function's priorities. It becomes hard to challenge decisions, hard to escalate concerns, and hard to speak about systemic issues that reflect poorly on the reporting chain. This is not always intentional. It is how organizations behave under pressure.

The goal is a structure that gives risk independence without making it an outsider.

The IIA's Three Lines Model is useful here, even outside internal audit, because it clarifies how governance works when roles are healthy (IIA, 2020). Management owns risk and controls. Functions that provide expertise and support help management manage risk. Independent assurance (internal audit) provides objective evaluation. Risk management typically lives in that middle space: supporting, coordinating, facilitating, setting standards, and helping leaders see the full risk picture, while not owning every operational control.

When your reporting line blurs those roles, you create confusion and conflict.

Common Reporting Structures and What They Get Right (and Wrong)

Reporting to Finance or the CFO

This is common in organizations where claims costs, insurance, and risk financing are the loudest parts of the risk portfolio. The advantages are real. Finance often has strong analytical discipline, visibility into cost drivers, and influence over budgeting. If you want resources for controls, Finance can be a powerful ally.

The risk is also real: the function that measures success in dollars may prioritize cost control in ways that unintentionally narrow the scope of risk conversations. Risk becomes "claims management" instead of "risk governance." You can end up optimizing short-term claim reductions while missing longer-term operational exposures, reputational risks, or safety culture issues that are not immediately visible on a ledger.

In public sector settings, this can show up when risk management becomes synonymous with insurance renewals, certificates, and TPA meetings. Those tasks matter, but they are not the whole mission.

If risk reports to Finance, the governance design needs strong, formal connection to operations and leadership decision forums, or risk becomes financially competent and operationally distant.

Reporting to Human Resources

This is common when workers' compensation, leave management, accommodations, training, and employee relations are central to the risk program. HR can be a natural home when risk is heavily people-centered and when the organization wants tight integration between safety practices and workforce practices.

The problem is that HR also owns sensitive outcomes: discipline, grievances, and sometimes investigations. That creates a perception issue. Frontline employees may not report near misses, close calls, or procedural drift if they believe reporting routes information toward corrective action that feels punitive. Psychological safety, which is crucial for early reporting, can suffer when employees believe "risk reporting" is effectively "HR reporting."

There is another practical issue: HR often carries a heavy workload and tends to be reactive because the issues are urgent and human. Risk management needs some reactive capability, but it also needs time and oxygen for prevention work. Under HR, risk can drift into a constant cycle of responding rather than designing controls.

If risk reports to HR, the organization should be deliberate about separating learning-focused reporting from disciplinary pathways, and it should establish clear just-culture boundaries that protect reporting while still maintaining accountability.

Reporting to Legal or the City/General Counsel

Legal has a strong understanding of liability, regulatory exposure, and litigation patterns. Legal also sees the organization through the lens of defensibility, which can improve documentation quality, contract terms, and investigative rigor.

But legal reporting lines can create two problems.

First, the organization can become risk-averse in the wrong way, focusing on what is defensible on paper rather than what is safe and effective in practice. Second, legal privilege concerns can unintentionally reduce transparency. Risk management relies on information flow. If risk conversations become constrained or overly guarded, learning slows down, and the workforce feels excluded.

Legal is an important partner. Whether legal should be the primary reporting line depends on whether the organization wants risk primarily as a protective shield or as an operational improvement engine. Most organizations need both, but the emphasis changes the culture.

Reporting to Operations or the COO

This option has an attractive logic: risk belongs where risk lives, which is in the work. Reporting into operations can give risk immediate access to what is happening in the field, faster adoption of controls, and better integration with supervisors and managers who actually implement change.

The risk is capture. Operations is under constant pressure to deliver service, meet schedules, and keep things moving. Under that pressure, risk can become negotiable. Risk managers may find themselves trimming recommendations to avoid slowing work down, or risk issues may get reframed as "operational challenges" without the governance weight they deserve.

This is where organizations unintentionally teach a dangerous lesson: "We will deal with risk when it is convenient." That is a governance failure, not a personal failure.

If risk reports to operations, it needs a strong escalation and oversight mechanism that allows it to speak beyond operational priorities when necessary.

Reporting to the CEO, City Manager, Superintendent, or Chief Administrative Officer

This structure often provides the best balance of independence and influence, especially when risk is expected to be enterprise-wide rather than limited to a narrow scope. When risk reports to the top administrative leader, it signals that risk is a leadership function, not a support function.

It also makes cross-department coordination easier. Risk rarely respects org charts. The biggest exposures often sit at boundaries: facilities and IT, HR and operations, procurement and project management, public interaction, and security. A reporting line to the top creates a natural mandate to convene and coordinate across those boundaries.

The challenge is that top leaders are busy. If the risk manager reports to the CEO or City Manager but has no structured rhythm for decision-making, the relationship can become sporadic. Risk needs governance mechanisms that keep it on the agenda: a risk committee, a standing quarterly ERM discussion, executive dashboards that focus on decisions, and escalation pathways that are used consistently.

When this model works, risk becomes a strategic partner rather than a transactional service.

Reporting to a Board Committee or Audit Committee

In many organizations, internal audit reports functionally to the audit committee, which is designed to protect independence. Risk management is different from internal audit, but the idea of independent oversight is still useful.

A pure "risk reports to the board" model is less common operationally because risk work requires day-to-day integration and decision support. Still, many organizations benefit from formal board or committee visibility into the risk function, especially for enterprise-level risks.

A hybrid model often works best: risk reports administratively to executive leadership (for day-to-day influence) and has a formal dotted-line relationship to an audit committee, risk committee, or governing board for periodic reporting, escalation, and independence reinforcement. This mirrors the idea that governance bodies set expectations and receive risk information while management owns execution (COSO, 2017; IIA, 2020).

The Public-Sector Reality: Politics, Transparency, and Operational Complexity

In city governments, school districts, and public agencies, the reporting line question is more complex because governance is layered. You have elected boards or councils, appointed executives, public transparency expectations, and often strong labor dynamics. You also have mission pressure: services cannot simply stop because risk controls are inconvenient.

That environment makes internal control frameworks like the GAO Green Book especially relevant. The Green Book emphasizes management's responsibility for internal control throughout the entity and across functions, not just in one department (GAO, 2025). It frames internal control as a system designed to help agencies achieve objectives in operations, reporting, and compliance. Risk governance is a cousin of that concept: it is how the organization ensures that goals are pursued without avoidable harm, waste, or preventable failure.

For public sector risk managers, governance design has to address three practical realities:

First, risk must be able to escalate concerns without becoming political theater. Second, risk must partner with labor and frontline leadership in a way that encourages reporting rather than suppresses it. Third, risk must stay close to operational decision points because public service is operationally intense.

That is why the "top administrative leader plus formal oversight" model often fits public agencies well. It supports enterprise coordination without losing operational relevance.

A Practical Decision Framework: How to Choose the Right Reporting Line

Rather than chasing a universal answer, organizations should evaluate structure against a few criteria.

What is the primary role you expect risk management to play?

If your risk function is primarily insurance and claims administration, Finance may be a good fit. If the role is primarily workplace injury prevention tied to workforce systems, HR might fit. If the role is primarily litigation defense and regulatory response, Legal might fit.

But if your goal is enterprise risk governance, meaning seeing risks across silos, advising leaders on tradeoffs, and building controls into planning and operations, risk needs a reporting line that is not limited to one functional lens (COSO, 2017; ISO, 2018).

Does the reporting line create conflicts of interest?

A simple test: will the risk manager routinely evaluate, challenge, or recommend changes to the same function that signs their performance review?

If yes, you are building structural pressure toward silence or dilution. That does not mean it cannot work, but it means you need compensating controls: formal escalation rights, board visibility, documented independence expectations, and shared performance metrics that include enterprise outcomes.

Can the risk function influence resource allocation?

Risk recommendations often require money, staffing, or operational changes. If the reporting line does not connect risk to budgeting and prioritization, risk becomes "advice" with no traction.

This is why reporting to top administration often helps. It reduces the number of layers between risk insight and resource decisions.

Can the risk function maintain trust with frontline employees?

If reporting pathways are perceived as disciplinary or political, reporting collapses. The reporting line should support a culture where concerns travel upward early. That means the structure must reinforce learning, fairness, and transparency.

Is there a formal oversight mechanism?

A dotted-line relationship to a board committee, audit committee, or executive risk steering group creates a place where risk can be discussed beyond day-to-day operational pressure (IIA, 2020). That oversight does not replace executive reporting, but it strengthens independence and creates predictable escalation.

What a Strong Governance Model Looks Like in Practice

A strong model usually includes these pieces, regardless of where the risk manager reports:

A clear risk management charter that defines authority, scope, and responsibilities, aligned with the organization's governance expectations (COSO, 2017; ISO, 2018).

A consistent executive rhythm: quarterly enterprise risk reviews, or monthly risk snapshots that focus on decisions, not long updates. A cross-functional risk committee that includes operations, HR, finance, legal, and IT, designed to surface cross-boundary risks and track mitigation progress. Defined escalation pathways for high-severity issues, including how issues reach the CEO/City Manager and how they reach governing bodies when appropriate. Measurement that reflects prevention and control of health, not just lagging outcomes.

A relationship with internal audit that is collaborative but not confused. Internal audit provides independent assurance. Risk coordinates and supports management's risk practices. The Three Lines model helps keep those roles clear (IIA, 2020).

In public agencies, adding a structured tie to the governing board's audit committee or finance committee can be particularly useful, not as a workaround, but as a transparency mechanism that strengthens credibility.

My Recommendation: A Balanced Reporting Model That Works in Most Organizations

If the organization wants risk management to be enterprise-wide and not limited to claims, the strongest default is usually this:

Risk reports administratively to the top administrative executive (CEO, City Manager, Superintendent, CAO, or COO, depending on structure), with a formal dotted-line reporting relationship to a governing committee or equivalent oversight forum. The risk manager also maintains strong working partnerships with Finance, HR, Legal, and Operations through a risk steering process.

This model protects risk's ability to speak across silos, keeps it close to decision-makers, and creates an oversight path that reinforces independence and escalation when pressure rises (COSO, 2017; IIA, 2020; ISO, 2018; GAO, 2025).

Is it perfect? No. The fundamental determinant is how leaders behave. But structure either supports good behavior or makes good behavior harder. This model tends to make the right behaviors easier.

Closing

Risk management governance is not about org-chart aesthetics. It is about whether the organization can tell itself the truth early enough to prevent harm, control cost, and protect service delivery. When risk sits too low or too narrowly, enterprise blind spots grow. When risk sits too close to a single agenda, candor shrinks. The best reporting line is the one that allows risk to remain both honest and useful, independent and connected.

If you are reevaluating your structure, focus less on where risk has "always" lived and more on what you are asking the risk function to accomplish next. If you want risk to be a leadership discipline, position it where leadership decisions are made, and give it an oversight path that keeps it credible when pressure rises.

References

Committee of Sponsoring Organizations of the Treadway Commission. (2017). *Enterprise risk management: Integrating with strategy and performance*. COSO.

Government Accountability Office. (2025). *Standards for internal control in the federal government (Green Book)*. U.S. Government Accountability Office.

Institute of Internal Auditors. (2020). *The IIA's Three Lines Model: An update of the Three Lines of Defense*.

International Organization for Standardization. (2018). *ISO 31000:2018 Risk management: Guidelines*. ISO.

Chapter 9
The Risk Talent Lifecycle

Recruitment, Retention, and Role Rotation

The Risk Talent Lifecycle: Recruitment, Retention, and Role Rotation

The risk role is one of the easiest jobs to misunderstand and one of the hardest jobs to replace. That becomes painfully obvious the day a seasoned risk manager leaves, and the organization realizes how much of its memory lived in one person's head. Which carrier is actually responsive when the claim gets ugly? Which supervisors can coach safety without escalating a conflict? Which department always pushes back on corrective actions? Which vendor "meets the contract" but quietly creates risk? None of that is written down as cleanly as we pretend it is. Then the new person walks in, smart and capable, and still needs a year just to learn the unspoken map.

That experience is why talent has to be treated as part of risk governance, not an HR side task. If you want a stable risk program, you need a deliberate lifecycle: how you recruit, how you onboard, how you develop people, how you keep them, and how you rotate them without breaking continuity. The best organizations treat risk talent the way they treat risk controls: as something you design intentionally, monitor consistently, and improve over time (COSO, 2017; ISO, 2018). Engagement and retention data matter here, too, because risk teams do not operate in a vacuum. When engagement drops and people feel less connected to their organizations, retention challenges rise across the board, including in specialized roles such as risk and safety (Gallup, 2025a; Gallup, 2025b). At the same time, turnover is expensive, not only in recruiting costs but also in lost productivity and institutional knowledge, and even conservative estimates place replacement costs as a meaningful fraction of annual pay for many roles (SHRM, 2019).

Recruiting for Reality, Not for a Job Posting

Most risk job postings read like a wish list written by three different departments that never met. HR wants training and policy experience. Finance wants insurance and claims. Legal wants contract review and defensibility. Operations wants someone who can "fix safety" without slowing the work down. So the posting becomes a five-page document that demands 10 years of experience, certifications, deep analytics, conflict-resolution skills, and "other duties as assigned," which is usually code for "we have not decided what this role really is."

Recruitment starts with clarity. Before you post anything, you need to be honest about the risk portfolio. Is this role primarily risk financing and claims oversight, or is it enterprise risk governance, or is it operational safety and prevention, or is it a blended model? In many organizations it is blended, but the blend still needs priorities. COSO's ERM framework pushes the idea that risk management is about integrating risk with strategy and performance, not simply reacting to incidents. That implication matters for hiring because you are selecting for the capability to influence decisions, not just manage transactions (COSO, 2017).

When you hire without clarity, you either scare away strong candidates who can see the mismatch or attract candidates who accept the mismatch and then burn out trying to meet conflicting expectations.

A practical recruiting mindset looks like this:

You define the "non-negotiables" of the role in plain language. Not buzzwords, not abstract competencies, just what the person must be able to do in the first six months. You identify which skills are trainable versus which are foundational. You decide what kind of authority the role will actually have. And you align the reporting structure so the role is set up to succeed, not set up to be blamed later.

The other critical piece is how you interview. Risk hiring fails when interviews only test knowledge. The job is not just about knowledge. It is influence. It is judgment. It is the ability to communicate the uncomfortable truth without triggering defensiveness.

So interviews should include scenarios that reveal how candidates think and how they communicate. A good candidate can explain how they would handle a near miss that operations wants to bury, or a supervisor who is respected but repeatedly ignores controls, or a pattern of claims that suggests a systemic failure no one wants to name.

If you hire only for compliance and technical knowledge, you might get a person who can write a policy and run a claims review, but cannot move a culture. If you hire only for charisma and "people skills," you might get a person who is liked but cannot build durable controls. Risk needs both.

Onboarding That Builds Credibility Fast

Risk onboarding is often treated like a normal HR onboarding process, and that is a mistake. This role depends on trust, relationships, and organizational knowledge. A new risk manager can be technically excellent and still fail if they do not earn credibility with supervisors, unions, department heads, and finance partners early.

A strong onboarding plan is structured but human. It typically includes:

- Early listening sessions with operations, HR, finance, legal, and IT that focus on real pain points and how those groups define "risk."

- A claims and incident deep dive, not to judge the past, but to identify patterns and learn where the system is weak.
- A field immersion component so the risk leader sees the real work, real constraints, and real hazards, rather than learning the organization through reports.
- A clear 90-day deliverable that proves value without overpromising, something like a prioritized risk register, an action plan for top exposures, or a corrective action closure improvement process.

This is where governance supports talent. If risk is positioned properly, the organization will give the new leader access to decision-makers and space to learn. If risk is poorly positioned, the new leader will be stuck chasing signatures, fighting for data, and reacting to crises with no runway.

One more thing matters: transparency about what success looks like. The risk leader should not have to guess whether they are being judged on claims costs, incident rates, training completion, audit outcomes, or something else. Confusion here creates misaligned behavior. If you want prevention, you cannot reward only lagging metrics.

Retention Is a Governance Issue, Not a Perk Problem

When people leave risk roles, organizations often blame pay first. Compensation matters, but the deeper drivers are usually workload, lack of authority, lack of development, and the emotional grind of being the messenger. Gallup's work on engagement and retention themes points to culture, engagement, and wellbeing as major reasons people leave jobs, which aligns with what risk professionals experience when they are overloaded, isolated, or stuck in constant conflict (Gallup, 2025c). U.S. engagement data has also shown sustained weakness, which should be read as a warning sign for retention across roles, especially roles that sit in the middle of competing priorities (Gallup, 2025b).

Retention is also about cost. Even if you can replace the role, you are paying for the gap: time, productivity, continuity, and institutional knowledge. SHRM has long highlighted that turnover carries significant cost and that organizations should consider the full replacement and transition burden, not just recruiting fees (SHRM, 2019). For specialized roles like risk, the real cost is often amplified because relationships and organizational memory are part of the job.

So what keeps risk talent?

Reasonable workload and clear priorities

Risk teams burn out when they are expected to own everything. In many organizations, risk is treated like a catch-all for safety, claims, compliance, training, emergency management, business continuity, contracts, vendor risk, and whatever new regulatory issue shows up next week. No one can do that well without prioritization.

Retention improves when leadership chooses, explicitly, what risk will focus on and what it will not. That is not abandonment. That is strategy. It is also a signal of respect.

Authority that matches responsibility

If you make the risk leader responsible for outcomes but give them no authority to influence decisions, you create a guaranteed frustration loop. People will not stay in a role where they are blamed for things they cannot control.

This is where reporting structure and escalation rights matter. A risk leader who can surface issues, gain decisions, and secure resources is more likely to stay. A risk leader who is expected to fix systemic problems through persuasion alone, while being blocked by silos, will eventually leave.

Professional growth and a visible path forward

A common retention failure is that risk roles become a dead end. People enter, become experts, and then realize there is no clear next step other than leaving. MIT Sloan research and commentary on career advancement have reinforced a simple truth: people stay when they can see development and progression, not just stability (MIT Sloan Management Review, 2023).

In the public sector, this is especially relevant because classification structures can slow progression. That does not mean growth is impossible. It means you have to design it: rotational assignments, special projects, cross-functional leadership roles, mentoring, and formal development pathways. OPM's career development guidance reflects this broader concept of building career paths and development structures rather than expecting employees to "figure it out" on their own (OPM, n.d.).

Psychological safety and fair conflict

Risk work involves hard conversations. If those conversations routinely turn personal, political, or punitive, people will leave. If risk leaders feel they cannot speak plainly without career risk, they will either become quiet or they will exit. Psychological safety is not a soft concept here. It is a retention control.

Building the Risk Bench: Pipeline Thinking

If your risk program is built around one strong person, it is not a program. It is a dependency.

A talent lifecycle approach builds a bench. That includes cross-training, documented processes, and a plan for succession. It also includes a recruitment pipeline, which can be as simple as internships, analyst roles, and rotational assignments for high-potential employees from operations, finance, HR, or internal audit.

This is where the "Three Lines" concept, while originally framed around governance and assurance, can be useful for talent strategy. The model clarifies that risk is not owned by the risk department alone. Management owns risk in the first line, support functions provide expertise and oversight in the second line, and internal audit provides independent assurance in the third line (IIA, 2020). When organizations treat that structure seriously, they naturally create more places where risk capability can grow. Supervisors learn risk thinking. Analysts learn risk reporting. Managers learn controls. The bench gets stronger.

The strongest pipelines often come from inside the organization because internal candidates already understand the culture, the politics, and the operational reality. External hires still matter, especially when you need new capability, but internal development is usually the most reliable way to build continuity.

Role Rotation: Why It Helps and Why It Scares People

Role rotation is one of those ideas that sounds good until you imagine the transition. Risk work is relational and knowledge-heavy, so leaders worry that rotation will create instability.

That fear is valid. Rotation done carelessly can break continuity, weaken relationships, and create a revolving door of half-informed leaders. But rotation done deliberately can strengthen capability, reduce burnout, prevent capture, and even support internal control integrity.

There are three big reasons rotation belongs in this chapter.

Rotation fights stagnation and tunnel vision

After a few years in the same risk seat, the work can become repetitive. The same meetings. The same types of incidents. The same budget fights. Even strong people begin to accept the status quo. Rotation disrupts that. A leader moving into a new environment sees problems with fresh eyes. They also bring practices that worked elsewhere.

Rotation reduces "role capture"

Risk leaders sometimes become too embedded in one leadership team or one operational worldview. That is not corruption. It is human. Over time, you start to protect relationships, avoid conflict, and speak more gently about things you used to name directly.

Rotation reduces that risk. It resets the relationships. It also reinforces the idea that the risk role is a leadership discipline, not a personality-based arrangement.

Rotation supports internal control integrity and fraud deterrence

From an internal control perspective, rotating key responsibilities is a recognized control practice in many settings. Cornell's internal control guidance, for example, notes that rotating key control responsibilities can strengthen segregation of duties, reveal lapses, and cross-train others (Cornell University, n.d.). Fraud prevention discussions also commonly include cross-training, mandatory vacations, and job rotation as part of an environment of competence and oversight (ACFE, 2024).

That matters for risk functions because risk teams often control sensitive processes: claims management coordination, vendor oversight, safety investigations, corrective action tracking, and sometimes approval flows tied to insurance or settlements. Rotation and cross-coverage reduce the risk that "one person runs the whole thing" without visibility.

The Rotation Design: How to Do It Without Breaking the Program

Rotation should not be a surprise. It should be a system.

Here is what a responsible rotation model typically includes.

A defined time horizon that fits the role

Not every role rotates on the same timeline. Some roles need longer tenure because relationships and technical mastery matter. Others benefit from shorter cycles because they are high-pressure, conflict-heavy, and prone to burnout.

In practice, many organizations find that a multi-year cycle, long enough to deliver meaningful improvements but short enough to prevent stagnation, is a reasonable target. The specific number is less important than the discipline: make it predictable and plan for it.

Overlap and handoff as a formal requirement

If rotation is planned, overlap should be built into the model. The outgoing leader should transfer knowledge, introduce key relationships, and deliver a real transition brief that covers active risks, open corrective actions, political landmines, and what is not written down.

This is one place where leaders need to fund the transition. If you expect clean handoffs without overlap, you are choosing risk.

Documentation that reduces "tribal knowledge"

A healthy risk program does not depend on memory. It depends on documentation that is alive: playbooks, decision logs, claims escalation guides, vendor contact maps, committee charters, and risk register history.

This is not paperwork for its own sake. It is continuity infrastructure.

A bench strategy, not a single replacement

Rotation works best when the organization has a bench: deputies, analysts, or cross-trained partners who can step in. If you rotate a leader out and the only replacement is a cold external hire, you have built a fragile system.

Career benefits that make rotation a reward, not a punishment

Rotation fails when it feels like forced movement. It succeeds when it is clearly tied to development, promotion pathways, leadership exposure, and skill building.

OPM's broader approach to career development emphasizes structured paths and development opportunities that help employees progress and build competencies (OPM, n.d.). While not risk-specific, the principle is the same: people invest more when they can see that the organization is investing in them.

Retention Through Rotation: The Counterintuitive Truth

Some leaders avoid rotation because they think it will increase turnover. But in many organizations, the lack of development and mobility is what drives turnover. People leave to grow. They leave to learn. They leave to escape stagnation.

Career growth has been repeatedly linked to retention in both research and practice-oriented discussions. If risk roles have no path and no variety, your high performers will eventually walk. When structured well, rotation can be part of the retention strategy because it provides growth without exit.

The key is to make rotation part of a broader lifecycle: recruit with clarity, onboard with structure, develop with intention, retain with support, and rotate with continuity safeguards.

Special Considerations in Public Agencies and School Districts

Public-sector risk management has unique pressures:

- The work is public, so incidents become political.
- The workforce is diverse, often unionized, and spread across departments with very different risk profiles.
- Budgets are constrained and hiring cycles are slow.
- Leadership changes can be frequent, which destabilizes priorities.

These realities make talent planning even more important. When risk leaders leave in a public agency, replacement is often slower, and the consequences of gaps can be more visible.

Rotation can work well in public agencies when it is anchored in leadership development and cross-department exposure. The agency benefits when risk leaders understand operations deeply, and operations leaders understand risk thinking. But again, that requires structured handoffs and a bench.

Retention also requires protecting well-being. Risk roles in public-facing environments are often emotionally heavy because they deal with injuries, traumatic incidents, conflict, and scrutiny. If you want people to stay, you need staffing levels that allow them to breathe, not just survive.

A Practical Talent Lifecycle Model for Risk Teams

A strong risk talent lifecycle is not complicated, but it does require discipline.

Stage One: Attract and recruit

Clarify the mission, scope, authority, and success measures. Hire for influence and judgment, not just technical skill. Use scenario-based interviews that reveal how candidates communicate under pressure. Ground the role in enterprise priorities aligned with governance frameworks that emphasize integration and leadership accountability (COSO, 2017; ISO, 2018).

Stage Two: Onboard and integrate

Build credibility through listening, field immersion, and early wins that matter. Create a 90-day plan tied to real deliverables. Establish relationships across the organization early.

Stage Three: Develop and support

Provide training, mentorship, and cross-functional exposure. Create visible pathways for advancement. Support the emotional load of the work. Track leading indicators of burnout: workload, backlog, and constant crisis response.

Stage Four: Retain and recognize

Align responsibility with authority. Protect time for prevention work. Reward truth-telling and early reporting. Recognize that turnover is expensive and disruptive, especially for knowledge-heavy roles (SHRM, 2019).

Stage Five: Rotate and sustain

Plan rotations proactively with overlap, documentation, and bench strength. Use rotation as both a development tool and an internal control strengthener, not as a reaction to conflict. Include cross-training and rotation practices that reduce the concentration of knowledge and support control integrity (Cornell University, n.d.; ACFE, 2024).

Closing

Risk management is often described as a system, a set of controls, a framework, and governance. All true. But none of it is durable without people who can do the work and stay long enough to build momentum. Recruitment without clarity creates frustration. Onboarding without structure creates slow starts and credibility gaps. Retention without authority creates burnout. Rotation without continuity creates instability.

If you want a risk program that outlasts personalities, treat talent like risk. Design it, measure it, and keep improving it. Start by asking a few honest questions: Are we hiring for what this role truly is, or what we wish it could be? Do we have a bench, or do we have a dependency? Do we make it possible for risk leaders to succeed, or do we make them responsible for outcomes they cannot influence? And when it is time for someone to move on, do we have a transition that protects the organization, or do we just hope the next person figures it out?

Those answers will tell you whether your risk program is built on a person or built as a system.

References

Association of Certified Fraud Examiners. (2024). *Fraud prevention and risk management considerations*. Fraud Magazine.

Committee of Sponsoring Organizations of the Treadway Commission. (2017). *Enterprise risk management: Integrating with strategy and performance*. COSO.

Cornell University, Division of Financial Services. (n.d.). *Segregation of duties: Rotate job duties*. Cornell University.

Gallup. (2025a). *State of the Global Workplace 2025*. Gallup.

Gallup. (2025b). *U.S. employee engagement sinks to a 10-year low*. Gallup.

Gallup. (2025c). *Global indicator: Employee retention and attraction*. Gallup.

Institute of Internal Auditors. (2020). *The IIA's Three Lines Model: An update of the Three Lines of Defense*. The IIA.

International Organization for Standardization. (2018). *ISO 31000:2018 Risk management: Guidelines*. ISO.

MIT Sloan Management Review. (2023). *To keep employees, focus on career advancement*. MIT Sloan Management Review.

Society for Human Resource Management. (2019). *Reducing employee turnover with creative workplace solutions*. SHRM.

U.S. Office of Personnel Management. (n.d.). *Career development*. OPM.

Chapter 10
Crisis Leadership and Organizational Resilience

Leading When the Plan No Longer Fits the Moment

Crisis Leadership and Organizational Resilience: Leading When the Plan No Longer Fits the Moment

Every organization loves a plan until the moment the plan no longer matches reality. That moment is the start of a real crisis. Not the kind that shows up neatly in a tabletop exercise, but the kind that forces leaders to make decisions with incomplete information, strained resources, and a public that wants answers now. In those moments, the binder does not lead. People do. And the uncomfortable truth is that crisis leadership is rarely about executing the perfect playbook. It is about stabilizing the system long enough to learn what is actually happening, then adjusting faster than the situation changes.

Most leaders are trained to manage operations. Crisis leadership is different. It is leadership under uncertainty, with consequences that compound quickly. It forces tradeoffs that feel unfair. It exposes gaps you did not know you had. It also reveals what kind of organization you really built on ordinary days, because resilience is not something you "activate." It is something you either have in your habits, your relationships, and your decision pathways, or you do not (Weick & Sutcliffe, 2007; Duchek, 2020). When the plan no longer fits, the question becomes simple and brutal: can you still coordinate, communicate, and decide without losing trust, safety, and purpose?

The purpose of this chapter is practical. It is about what leaders actually do when conditions change faster than procedures, when the chain of command is necessary but not sufficient, and when your best move is not to insist on control but to build shared understanding. Crisis leadership is sensemaking, coordination, and moral clarity under pressure (Weick, 1995; Boin et al., 2016).

Crisis leadership begins when everyday routines break, and your first job is to create shared understanding before you try to "fix" anything, because action without sensemaking often accelerates harm (Weick, 1995; Klein, 1998). Organizational resilience is not a motivational concept; it is a set of capabilities that can be built, including anticipating, monitoring, responding, and learning, and those capabilities show up most clearly in how leaders communicate, allocate authority, and close feedback loops (Hollnagel, 2014; Duchek, 2020). The organizations that hold together under stress protect psychological safety and information flow because silence, fear, and blame make small problems unmanageable crises (Edmondson, 1999; Westrum, 2004). Finally, the plan still matters, but only as a starting point; resilient leaders treat plans as hypotheses, adapt quickly, and learn in public without losing credibility (Boin et al., 2016; Weick & Sutcliffe, 2007).

When the Plan Stops Working, Sensemaking Becomes the Work

In a stable environment, leaders can focus on execution. In a crisis, leaders have to focus on meaning. That sounds abstract until you see how crises unfold in real time. Information arrives in fragments. Different departments hold different pieces of the truth. Rumors move faster than verified facts. People interpret the same event through different lenses, including legal exposure, operational impact, public perception, and personal fear. If leaders rush to action without building shared understanding, they often make the situation worse, not because they are careless, but because they are operating from the wrong story.

Karl Weick's work on sensemaking explains why this is so common. In disruption, people try to "make the world sensible" quickly, and the stories they build drive action (Weick, 1995). When leaders do not shape sensemaking, sensemaking still happens; it just happens informally, inconsistently, and often inaccurately. That creates fragmentation. Fragmentation is not simply inefficient in a crisis. It is dangerous.

A practical example arises in public agencies during severe weather or infrastructure failures. Facilities has one assessment, operations has another, communications has a third, and leadership is hearing all of them in separate conversations. Without a structured way to build a common operating picture, decisions become reactive and conflicting. One department announces closures while another is still operating. Staff get mixed directions. The public sees inconsistency and assumes incompetence. Trust drops. Now the crisis is not only operational. It is reputational.

The first leadership move is to slow down the story, not the response. That means asking, early and repeatedly: What do we know? What do we think we know? What do we not know yet? What is changing right now? Those questions sound simple, but they force a discipline that crisis environments punish. They also prevent "false certainty," which is one of the most common ways leaders lose credibility.

Sensemaking also requires a willingness to accept that initial interpretations will be wrong. Gary Klein's work on decision-making in natural settings shows how experienced leaders make rapid judgments based on patterns, but also how they test those judgments through cues and feedback (Klein, 1998). In crisis leadership, humility is not a personality trait. It is a risk control.

Adaptive Leadership When Technical Answers Are Not Enough

Many crises begin as technical problems and become adaptive problems. A power outage, a cyber incident, a violent incident, a sudden regulatory change, an outbreak, a major lawsuit, a catastrophic injury. The technical piece is important. But the crisis becomes "real" when the organization must change its behavior, priorities, and coordination patterns under stress.

Ron Heifetz and colleagues describe adaptive challenges as problems that cannot be solved by expertise alone. They require learning, value tradeoffs, and changes in how people work together (Heifetz et al., 2009). That is why "just follow the plan" is often insufficient. The plan was written for a version of reality that no longer exists.

A common trap is for leaders to try to turn adaptive challenges back into technical ones. They look for the one expert who can "handle it." They demand certainty. They insist on a single narrative too early. In doing so, they suppress dissenting information and reduce the organization's ability to see emerging risks.

Adaptive crisis leadership looks different. It includes a few behaviors that often feel counterintuitive:

- Leaders create space for disagreement, because disagreement is how weak signals survive.
- Leaders ask frontline staff what they are seeing, because the first accurate data often comes from the edges, not the center.
- Leaders name the tradeoffs honestly, because pretending tradeoffs do not exist is how trust collapses.
- Leaders keep the organization anchored to mission, because fear naturally pulls people toward self-protection and blame.

This does not mean leaders abdicate authority. It means leaders use authority to create learning and coordination, not just compliance.

Communication That Stabilizes, Not Just Updates

In a crisis, communication is not an add-on. It is the central mechanism of control. If communication is unclear, inconsistent, or evasive, the organization destabilizes. Staff fill gaps with assumptions. The public fills gaps with suspicion. Partners fill gaps with their own narratives. And the leadership team ends up managing second-order effects that were preventable.

Effective crisis communication has two audiences at the same time: internal and external. Internally, staff need clarity about priorities, roles, safety, and decision pathways. Externally, stakeholders need truthful information, a sense of direction, and confidence that the organization is not hiding. Crisis scholars emphasize that leadership credibility depends heavily on communication choices during high uncertainty, including transparency, timeliness, and consistency (Boin et al., 2016; Bundy et al., 2017).

A few communication practices matter more than people think:

Say what you know and what you do not know, plainly

Leaders lose credibility when they overpromise. If you do not know, say you do not know, then say when you will know more. This is not weakness. It is trust-building. It signals that the organization is committed to truth over image.

Create a predictable rhythm

In chaos, predictability calms the system. Set update rhythms. Even if the update is "no change," the rhythm matters. It reduces rumor velocity and helps staff plan.

Keep messages aligned across departments

One of the fastest ways to create reputational damage is conflicting messages from different parts of the organization. This is where governance matters. A crisis communications function should not be improvising in isolation. It should be connected to the core decision forum.

Communicate safety boundaries

Staff need to know what risks are acceptable and what are not. In some crises, the most important message is, "We are not asking you to do this if it is unsafe." In other crises, it is, "If you see X, stop and escalate immediately." These are operational controls delivered through communication.

Decision-Making Under Pressure: Authority, Speed, and the Reality of Uncertainty

Crisis leadership forces leaders to make decisions under imperfect conditions. That does not mean decisions should be reckless. It means that decision-making processes must be designed for speed without sacrificing judgment.

A helpful starting point is to accept that in crisis settings, the organization needs both centralized coordination and decentralized initiative. Too much centralization slows response and blinds leaders to real-time conditions. Too much decentralization creates fragmentation and competing priorities. High-reliability research describes this balance as a form of mindful organizing: leaders coordinate tightly around the mission while allowing flexibility at the front line (Weick & Sutcliffe, 2007).

Incident command systems exist for a reason. Studies of incident command structures show how temporary hierarchies and role clarity can support coordination in complex emergencies (Bigley & Roberts, 2001). However, systems are not magic. They work when leaders understand what they are for. Incident command is a framework for coordination and information flow, not a guarantee of good decisions.

Here are three decision disciplines that matter in most crises:

Define decision rights early

Who can make what decisions, at what thresholds, and how quickly? If decision rights are unclear, people either freeze or act inconsistently. In some crises, the worst outcome is not a wrong decision. It is no decision.

Use "good enough" decisions with feedback

Crisis decisions are often reversible. Leaders should treat them as experiments with feedback loops. Decide, act, assess, adjust. This is not indecision. It is adaptive control.

Track second-order effects

Many crisis mistakes come from focusing on the first problem and ignoring cascading impacts. For example, closing a facility may reduce immediate risk but create staffing overload elsewhere. Policy changes may reduce liability but increase operational complexity. Leaders need a habit of asking, "What does this decision create downstream?"

Situational awareness research emphasizes that awareness is built from perception, comprehension, and projection. Leaders must not only gather information but also understand what it means and anticipate where it is going (Endsley, 1995). That is not a luxury in crisis leadership. It is a core function.

Psychological Safety and Information Flow: The Difference Between Early Warning and Late Surprise

Most crisis failures have a problem with silence somewhere in the chain. Someone knew something. Someone saw something. Someone felt something was off. But the information did not travel upward, or it traveled too late, or it was softened until it lost urgency.

Psychological safety is the condition that allows people to speak up, admit mistakes, and challenge assumptions without fear of punishment or humiliation (Edmondson, 1999). In crisis environments, psychological safety becomes even more important because uncertainty is high and errors are more likely. If people are afraid of being blamed, they stop reporting the very information leaders need.

Westrum's typology of organizational cultures helps clarify why some organizations are resilient and others are brittle. In generative cultures, information flows freely, and failures are treated as opportunities to improve. In pathological cultures, messengers are punished, and failures are hidden (Westrum, 2004). Crisis conditions intensify whichever culture you already have.

A practical example: a school district experiences an escalation of incidents and a threat-related event. The safety plan exists, but staff hesitate to report earlier warning signs because prior reporting was dismissed or met with criticism. By the time leadership becomes aware, the incident has already moved into the public sphere. Now leadership is not only managing safety. They are managing community trust under scrutiny. The technical plan did not fail first. The information flow failed first.

Crisis leaders protect the flow of information by being explicit about how reporting will be handled. They thank people for bringing forward concerns. They do not punish early reporting. They separate learning from discipline. They create quick channels for escalation that do not require navigating bureaucracy in the moment.

This also connects to just culture thinking. If every error is treated as misconduct, people hide errors. If reckless behavior is ignored, people lose respect for leadership. The goal is consistent, fair responses that preserve learning while maintaining accountability (Reason, 1997; Dekker, 2012).

Resilience as a Capability: Anticipate, Monitor, Respond, Learn

Organizations often describe resilience as grit or toughness. That framing is incomplete. Resilience is not simply enduring hardship. It is the ability to adapt and recover while maintaining core function.

Erik Hollnagel describes resilience engineering as the capacity to succeed under varying conditions, supported by capabilities to anticipate, monitor, respond, and learn (Hollnagel, 2014). Duchek's work similarly frames organizational resilience as a process that includes anticipation, coping, and adaptation (Duchek, 2020). These ideas matter because they shift resilience from personality to design.

Anticipate

Anticipation is not prediction. It is preparation for plausible disruptions. It includes scenario planning, but it also includes examining near misses, weak signals, and operational fragility. High-reliability organizations maintain a "preoccupation with failure," not because they are pessimistic, but because they know small failures carry information (Weick & Sutcliffe, 2007).

Monitor

Monitoring is the discipline of staying connected to what is changing now. In crises, monitoring includes operational metrics, but it also includes listening to staff, watching workload, tracking resource strain, and noticing when systems start to wobble. Many crises become unmanageable because leaders lose visibility into frontline reality.

Respond

Response capability includes speed, coordination, and the ability to allocate resources under pressure. It also includes the willingness to adjust goals temporarily. Some leaders cling to normal performance metrics during a crisis and burn out their workforce. Resilient leaders reset priorities and protect sustainability.

Learn

Learning is the difference between "we survived" and "we improved." After-action reviews are not useful if they become blame sessions or if lessons never translate into changes. Learning requires closing loops: identify what failed, fix it, test it, and revisit it.

Learning also requires memory. One reason organizations repeat crises is that institutional memory is fragile. People rotate, retire, or leave, and the organization forgets what it learned. Resilience improves when learning is documented and embedded into systems, not stored in individuals.

Leading Across Systems: Partners, Vendors, and the Boundary Problem

Crises rarely respect organizational boundaries. Public agencies rely on partners. School districts rely on local law enforcement, behavioral health, and vendors. Healthcare systems rely on suppliers, staffing agencies, and community services. In many crises, the most painful failures happen at the boundaries, where responsibility is unclear and coordination is slow.

Crisis research emphasizes interorganizational coordination as a major determinant of outcomes, especially in public emergencies where multiple agencies must coordinate quickly (Comfort, 2007; Boin et al., 2016). In risk governance terms, that means resilience is partially external. Your resilience depends on the reliability of your partners and the clarity of your agreements.

Practical resilience includes:

- Clear roles and escalation pathways with partners before crisis.
- Joint exercises that reflect real constraints.
- Shared communication protocols to prevent conflicting messages.
- Contract language and vendor expectations that include crisis performance, not just normal delivery.

Many organizations discover in crisis that their vendor relationships are purely transactional. Then the vendor fails, or simply cannot respond fast enough, and the organization has no alternatives. That is not bad luck. That is a governance gap.

What Crisis Leaders Actually Do in the First Hours

The first hours of a crisis are different from the rest. They require a specific kind of discipline.

Strong crisis leaders tend to do a few things early, consistently:

- They establish a decision forum quickly, even if the team is small at first.

- They stabilize people, not just systems, by naming priorities and protecting safety.
- They create a single source of truth for updates, even if information is incomplete.
- They assign roles that match the moment, not titles on paper.
- They protect the organization from "panic busy," where people do a lot of activity that does not reduce risk.

They also focus on what matters most: life safety, critical services, and trust. Many operational choices can be corrected later. Lost trust is harder to recover. Lost safety cannot be undone.

Closing

Crisis leadership is not about having a perfect plan. It is about leading when your plan is no longer enough. That requires sensemaking before certainty, coordination before heroics, and communication that stabilizes rather than performs. It also requires a clear moral center. People can tolerate uncertainty. They struggle to tolerate leaders who feel evasive, inconsistent, or indifferent to the human cost.

If you want to build organizational resilience, start by looking at your habits on ordinary days. Do people speak up early? Do leaders close loops? Do decisions get made with clarity and follow-through? Do partners know how to coordinate with you under stress? Those ordinary habits become your crisis performance.

A final reflection worth holding onto: in a crisis, you are not only managing an event. You are teaching your organization what it means to trust leadership. The way you listen, decide, and communicate in the moment becomes a long memory. Lead with truth, protect information flow, and treat the plan as a living tool. Then, when the moment stops matching the binder, your organization still knows how to move.

References

Bigley, G. A., & Roberts, K. H. (2001). The incident command system: High-reliability organizing for complex and volatile task environments. *Academy of Management Journal, 44*(6), 1281–1299.

Boin, A., 't Hart, P., Stern, E., & Sundelius, B. (2016). *The politics of crisis management: Public leadership under pressure* (2nd ed.). Cambridge University Press.

Bundy, J., Pfarrer, M. D., Short, C. E., & Coombs, W. T. (2017). Crises and crisis management: Integration, interpretation, and research development. *Journal of Management, 43*(6), 1661–1692.

Comfort, L. K. (2007). Crisis management in hindsight: Cognition, communication, coordination, and control. *Public Administration Review, 67*(S1), 189–197.

Dekker, S. (2012). *Just culture: Balancing safety and accountability* (2nd ed.). Ashgate.

Duchek, S. (2020). Organizational resilience: A capability-based conceptualization. *Business Research, 13*(1), 215–246.

Edmondson, A. C. (1999). Psychological safety and learning behavior in work teams. *Administrative Science Quarterly, 44*(2), 350–383.

Endsley, M. R. (1995). Toward a theory of situation awareness in dynamic systems. *Human Factors, 37*(1), 32–64.

Heifetz, R. A., Grashow, A., & Linsky, M. (2009). *The practice of adaptive leadership: Tools and tactics for changing your organization and the world.* Harvard Business Press.

Hollnagel, E. (2014). *Safety-I and Safety-II: The past and future of safety management.* Ashgate.

Klein, G. (1998). *Sources of power: How people make decisions.* MIT Press.

Reason, J. (1997). *Managing the risks of organizational accidents.* Ashgate.

Weick, K. E. (1995). *Sensemaking in organizations.* Sage.

Weick, K. E., & Sutcliffe, K. M. (2007). *Managing the unexpected: Resilient performance in an age of uncertainty* (2nd ed.). Jossey-Bass.

Westrum, R. (2004). A typology of organisational cultures. *Quality & Safety in Health Care, 13*(Suppl 2), ii22–ii27.

Part: IV – Data, Technology, and Human Decision- Making

Chapter 11
Data-Driven Decision Making in Risk Management

From Gut Feel to Evidence You Can Defend

Data-Driven Decision Making in Risk Management: From Gut Feel to Evidence You Can Defend

Most risk leaders have had the same frustrating experience. You raise a concern that feels obvious to you, you have years of pattern recognition behind it, and still, the room looks at you like you brought an opinion to a budget meeting. Then someone asks the question that changes everything: "Do we have data?" If the answer is no, the conversation drifts. If the answer is yes, the conversation sharpens. People may still disagree, but now they are disagreeing about evidence rather than instinct.

Here is the catch. Risk management cannot be only about data. It also cannot be only a gut feel. The job is to make decisions under uncertainty, and uncertainty does not disappear because you created a dashboard. What data does is give you defensible ground. It helps you explain why you made a choice, why you spent money, why you escalated a concern, and why you asked people to change behavior. It also helps you see patterns that no one person can reliably hold in their head, especially across departments, job classes, sites, and years (ISO, 2018; COSO, 2017).

The key learnings for this chapter come down to a few practical truths. Data does not replace judgment, but it does improve judgment when it is relevant, timely, and tied to decisions. Good risk data starts with definitions and governance, because inconsistent inputs create confident nonsense. The most useful metrics are those that track control health and system strain, not only outcomes after harm occurs. Analytics matter only if they lead to action, and action sustains only if leaders build feedback loops that show whether changes actually worked. Finally, evidence is only defensible when it is ethically collected, transparently interpreted, and communicated in a way that respects the people behind the numbers (Kahneman, 2011; ISO, 2018; COSO, 2017).

Why "Gut Feel" Fails in Modern Risk Work

There is a reason experienced leaders trust their instincts. In many environments, intuition is built from years of exposure to patterns. But intuition has limits. It is personal, inconsistent across leaders, and vulnerable to bias. Two smart people can look at the same situation and "feel" different conclusions. That does not make either person dishonest. It makes them human.

Daniel Kahneman describes how we rely on fast thinking that feels effortless and confident, even when the underlying judgment is incomplete or skewed by cognitive shortcuts (Kahneman, 2011). In risk management, those shortcuts show up all the time. A recent dramatic incident makes leaders overestimate its probability. An extended period without a major loss creates a false sense of safety. A charismatic manager can convince leadership that controls are strong, even if the data says compliance is weak. People remember the story that is easiest to recall, not the pattern that is statistically true.

Gut feel also struggles with scale. A risk manager might notice a trend in one division, but miss how the same trend is playing out across multiple sites. A supervisor might believe injuries are "just bad luck" until data shows the same body part is getting injured in the same task again and again. Data does not eliminate disagreement, but it compresses the debate toward reality.

None of this means leaders should abandon judgment. Risk management is not a math problem. It is a decision problem. The goal is to combine human judgment with evidence, then make choices you can defend to employees, executives, boards, regulators, and the public.

What "Data-Driven" Actually Means in Risk Management

"Data-driven" is one of those phrases that can become empty if we do not define it. In risk management, it should mean something specific: decisions are informed by evidence that is relevant to the risk, reliable enough to trust, and presented in a way that supports action.

COSO frames enterprise risk management as integrated with strategy and performance, implying that risk data should be connected to objectives, decisions, and outcomes rather than tracked as a separate reporting exercise (COSO, 2017). ISO 31000 emphasizes that risk management should be integrated, structured, comprehensive, and dynamic, which is another way of saying the information should help the organization adapt as conditions change (ISO, 2018).

So, data-driven risk management is not just counting incidents. It includes:

- Understanding exposure, such as hours worked, miles driven, patient days, student interactions, service calls, and public-facing contacts.

- Tracking control health, such as training completion with competency checks, preventive maintenance completion, corrective action closure time, inspection quality, and supervisor field contacts.

- Monitoring system strain, such as staffing vacancy rates, overtime, backlog, equipment downtime, and workload spikes.

- Measuring outcomes, such as injury rates, claims frequency and severity, near misses, property losses, and service disruptions.

- Capturing qualitative signals, such as employee reports, safety committee feedback, and customer or community complaints.

Data-driven does not mean "more data." It means decision-grade data.

Start With the Basics: Data You Can Trust Is Defined Data

Before you build a dashboard, you need agreements. What counts as a near miss? What counts as a first aid case? What counts as "training complete"? Is a corrective action "closed" when it is assigned, when it is completed, or when it is verified? These questions sound boring until you realize that inconsistent definitions create misleading trends.

If one division reports every near miss and another reports none, you do not have a safety comparison. You have a reporting culture comparison. If one supervisor marks training complete when employees attend, and another marks it complete only after a skills check, your training completion rate is not a real measure of competence.

This is why data governance is not a luxury. It is the foundation.

A practical risk data governance approach includes a short list of agreed definitions, a consistent way to collect and store the information, and a quality check process. It also includes clarity on ownership. Who owns the data, who verifies it, and who is accountable for correcting it when it is wrong?

This is where many risk programs stumble. They invest in software first and discover later that the data feeding it is messy. The software does not fix the mess. It displays it faster.

Leading Indicators, Lagging Indicators, and the Metrics That Actually Change Behavior

Most organizations over-rely on lagging indicators: injury rates, claim costs, lost-time days, and incident counts. Those measures matter, but they describe the past. They also invite underreporting when leaders reward "good numbers" without asking whether the controls are healthy.

A more mature approach balances lagging indicators with leading indicators. Leading indicators are measures of the activities and conditions that prevent losses. They are not perfect, but they are actionable. They tell you what to do next week, not what you should have done last year.

Examples of decision-grade leading indicators include:

- Corrective action closure time, especially overdue items and repeat findings.

- Preventive maintenance completion rates on critical equipment.

- Quality of inspections, not just quantity, meaning whether hazards are actually identified and controls are assigned.

- Supervisor field contact frequency with coaching notes.

- Safety committee action completion rates.

- Training competency checks, not just attendance.

If you have to choose a small set, choose measures that track whether your controls are alive. That idea aligns with the internal control view of organizations. Controls are not "present" because they exist in a document. They are present when they operate consistently and are monitored (COSO, 2013; GAO, 2014).

A subtle but important point: metrics do not just measure performance. They shape performance. People do what gets measured, especially what gets measured publicly. If you measure only injuries, you can accidentally create incentives to hide injuries. If you measure corrective action closure and verify completion, you create incentives to fix problems.

Evidence You Can Defend: Risk Quantification Without Pretending to Predict the Future

Risk quantification can be useful, but it becomes dangerous when it creates false precision. Leaders love numbers, and risk professionals sometimes feel pressure to provide them. The problem is that risk is uncertainty. When you pretend your model predicts the future with certainty, you teach leaders the wrong lesson.

A defensible approach to quantification focuses on ranges and scenarios. What is the likely range of loss? What are plausible worst cases? What is the cost of doing nothing?

What is the expected impact if we implement a control? These are decision questions, not prediction questions.

You can quantify risk in a few practical ways:

- Frequency and severity analysis of claims over time, adjusted for exposure.

- Cost of risk metrics, including retained losses, premiums, administrative cost, and prevention investment.

- Scenario analysis for high-impact events, such as a major facility loss, cyber incident, or violent incident.

- Control-effectiveness estimates, such as expected reduction in incidents after engineering changes, process redesign, or training with competency validation.

Good quantification also includes a plain-language explanation of assumptions. Executives and boards do not need a math lecture. They need to know what the numbers depend on and what could change them.

Turning Data Into Decisions: Dashboards That Answer Real Questions

A dashboard is not a scoreboard. It is a decision tool. The best dashboards answer a small set of questions that leaders actually need to manage risk.

A useful risk dashboard often answers questions like these:

- Where are losses occurring, and what patterns repeat?

- Which controls are failing or drifting?

- Where is system strain increasing?

- What corrective actions are overdue, and why?

- What decisions do leaders need to make this month?

That means your dashboard should not be a wall of charts. It should be a few indicators tied to decisions, with the ability to drill down when needed.

One practical approach is to separate the dashboard into three layers:

- A top layer for leadership, focused on a small number of indicators tied to enterprise priorities.

- A middle layer for managers, focused on control health and corrective actions.
- A frontline layer focused on local hazards, tasks, and immediate prevention actions.

When leaders ask for "more data," what they usually mean is "help me understand what matters." That is not achieved through volume. It is achieved through clarity.

Data Storytelling: The Skill Risk Leaders Need to Develop

Even good data fails if it is communicated poorly. Risk leaders often show charts that make sense to them and confuse everyone else. Or they present data without a narrative, and the group ends up debating the chart instead of addressing the risk.

A defensible risk narrative usually includes four pieces:

What is happening, stated clearly.
Why it matters, tied to mission, cost, safety, service delivery, and trust.
What is driving it, based on patterns, not guesses.
What decision is needed, including options and tradeoffs.

This is where risk leaders move from being analysts to being decision partners. Your job is not to "report." Your job is to help leaders decide.

A quick example: If a city sees rising vehicle claims, the narrative should not be "vehicle claims are up 18 percent." The narrative should connect the trend to exposure and root causes. Are miles driven increasing? Are certain units driving older vehicles? Is overtime up and fatigue showing? Is preventive maintenance behind? Are driver training and coaching consistent? Then the decision: do we invest in maintenance, adjust schedules, add coaching, replace vehicles, change routes, or accept the risk?

Data becomes persuasive when it is connected to reality and choices.

Predictive Analytics, AI, and the Temptation to Automate Judgment

Predictive analytics and AI can help risk programs spot patterns earlier, but they introduce new risks: overreliance, bias, and false confidence. If the model is trained on biased data or incomplete data, it can reinforce existing inequities and blind spots. If leaders treat the model as objective truth, they can stop asking the questions that keep systems safe.

This is not a reason to avoid analytics. It is a reason to use it responsibly. The most mature approach treats models as tools that support human judgment, not replace it.

A responsible approach includes:

- Clear documentation of what the model is designed to do and what it is not designed to do.

- Ongoing validation against real outcomes.

- Human review before decisions that impact people, especially employment actions, discipline, and access.

- Privacy protections and data minimization, especially when data includes employee or community information.

Risk leaders should also be cautious about using analytics as a proxy for leadership. No model can compensate for poor supervision, unclear procedures, or under-resourced operations. Data can reveal those problems. It cannot fix them.

Data Ethics and Trust: People Are Not Just Data Points

Risk data often includes sensitive information: injury details, medical information, employee performance notes, incident investigations, security events, and sometimes community interactions. If people believe data is being used to punish rather than improve, reporting collapses, and your data becomes less accurate.

This is where psychological safety connects to data strategy. When employees trust that reporting leads to learning and fair action, they report more. When they fear punishment, they report less. A risk program that wants good data must protect the environment that produces it (Edmondson, 1999; Westrum, 2004).

Data ethics in risk management should include:

- Clear communication about how data will be used.

- Limits on access, with role-based permissions.

- Avoiding "gotcha" metrics that target individuals without context.

- Using data to improve systems, not to shame people.

- Strong privacy practices and compliance with applicable laws and policies.

Trust is a control. When trust fails, your information flow fails, and risk becomes harder to manage.

Common Failure Modes in Data-Driven Risk Programs

Organizations often repeat the same mistakes when they try to "go data-driven."

Measuring what is easy, not what is meaningful

Training completion is easy to measure. Competency is harder. Inspections completed are easy. Inspection quality is harder. Meetings held are easy. Corrective actions closed is harder. Easy measures can become a comfort blanket while the real control over health remains unknown.

Ignoring exposure

An increase in incidents may reflect increased exposure, not worse performance. Without exposure, you risk false alarms or false reassurance.

Building dashboards with no decision owner

If no one owns the decision the data is intended to support, the dashboard becomes a monthly ritual rather than a management tool.

Confusing correlation with cause

A spike in incidents near a schedule change might be linked, but it needs investigation. Data should trigger questions, not declare conclusions.

Using data as punishment

The fastest way to destroy reporting is to use data to punish individuals without fairness or context. The data becomes less accurate, and the culture becomes more silent.

Case Examples: What This Looks Like in Practice

Public sector operations

A city notices a steady rise in strain injuries among maintenance staff. The initial instinct is to blame technique and schedule refresher training. The data story reveals something else: overtime increased, staffing vacancies rose, and preventive maintenance fell behind, which increased manual handling and rushed work. The decision becomes less about "train harder" and more about resource allocation, task redesign, equipment upgrades, and realistic workload. Training still matters, but it is no longer the only control.

Education settings

A school district sees increased incidents related to student behavior. The data is not just discipline referrals. It includes where incidents occur, time of day, staffing ratios, and what supports were present. The pattern shows higher incident rates during transitions and in specific areas with weak supervision lines. The decision becomes environment design, staffing coverage, consistent protocols, and targeted support, not just reactive consequences.

Healthcare environments

A facility experiences an increase in patient-handling injuries. Data shows unit-specific patterns and peak times. It also shows equipment downtime and inconsistent lift availability. The decision becomes equipment maintenance, lift accessibility, workflow redesign, and competency checks, not just annual training.

The theme is consistent: evidence shifts the conversation from blame to systems.

Building the Capability: A Practical Approach to Becoming More Evidence-Based

Most organizations do not need a massive analytics team to improve. They need discipline.

A realistic build plan often looks like this:

First, define the small set of enterprise risk questions leadership needs answered, and align metrics to those questions.
Second, standardize definitions and data collection to ensure your data is trustworthy.
Third, build a simple dashboard that focuses on decisions and controls health, then iterate based on how leaders actually use it.
Fourth, build routines for review, such as monthly risk control reviews and quarterly enterprise risk discussions tied to strategic priorities (COSO, 2017; ISO, 2018).
Fifth, develop the skill of communication and narrative, because the best analysis still fails if it cannot move decisions.
Finally, protect trust and ethics, because data quality depends on the culture that produces the data.

You will know you are improving when leaders stop asking for more charts and start asking better questions, and when corrective actions close faster because the organization can see where controls are breaking.

Closing

Data-driven decision-making in risk management is not about replacing experience. It is about sharpening it. It is about moving from "I feel like this is risky" to "Here is what is happening, here is the pattern, here is why it matters, and here is what we need to decide." That kind of evidence does more than persuade. It protects. It protects the workforce because controls get fixed earlier. It protects leadership because decisions become defensible. It protects the organization because resources get allocated to the risks that actually matter.

If you want one simple standard, make it this: data should lead to action, and action should be measured for effectiveness. If your data does not change decisions, it is noise. If your decisions are not followed by measurement, you are guessing. The goal is not perfection. The goal is defensible progress, built on evidence you can explain and stand behind.

References

Committee of Sponsoring Organizations of the Treadway Commission. (2013). *Internal control: Integrated framework*. COSO.

Committee of Sponsoring Organizations of the Treadway Commission. (2017). *Enterprise risk management: Integrating with strategy and performance*. COSO.

Government Accountability Office. (2014). *Standards for internal control in the federal government (Green Book)*. U.S. Government Accountability Office.

International Organization for Standardization. (2018). *ISO 31000:2018 Risk management: Guidelines*. ISO.

Kahneman, D. (2011). *Thinking, fast and slow*. Farrar, Straus and Giroux.

Westrum, R. (2004). A typology of organisational cultures. *Quality & Safety in Health Care, 13*(Suppl 2), ii22–ii27.

Edmondson, A. C. (1999). Psychological safety and learning behavior in work teams. *Administrative Science Quarterly, 44*(2), 350–383.

Chapter 12
Technology in Risk Management – Systems, Sensors, and Cyber

Tools That Help (and Hurt) When Things Get Real

Tools That Help (and Hurt) When Things Get Real

Technology has become the quiet partner in almost every risk decision. Sometimes it's obvious, like a cyber alert or a camera feed. More often it's invisible: a workflow that decides who gets notified, a spreadsheet that drives budget choices, a claims system that shapes how losses are coded, a maintenance platform that decides whether a work order gets done this week or next month. In calm periods, those systems feel like "support." In a real event, they become the environment you're operating inside. If the environment is poorly designed, you feel it immediately.

This chapter is about the promise and the trap. Technology can make risk management faster, more consistent, and more defensible. It can also create blind spots, false confidence, and new categories of risk that didn't exist before you installed the tool. The problem is not that risk leaders buy technology. The problem is when organizations confuse technology with control, or mistake data capture for insight, or treat a dashboard like a substitute for leadership.

A healthy approach starts with a simple stance: tools should support decisions, protect people, and strengthen resilience. If a tool makes the organization less honest, less responsive, or less safe, it is not a "modernization." It is a liability wearing a progress badge. Risk leaders need the ability to evaluate tech like a risk decision, not like a shopping decision.

The key learnings for this chapter come down to a few practical truths. Systems only work when definitions, workflows, and accountability are clear; otherwise, they just accelerate confusion. Sensors and wearables can reduce harm, but only when the organization is honest about privacy, false alarms, and how behavior changes under surveillance. Cybersecurity is no longer just an IT issue because a cyber incident can stop operations, compromise safety, and undermine public trust, especially in environments where operational technology and physical systems are involved (NIST, 2024; ISA, n.d.; Stouffer et al., 2015). Finally, incident response is not a document. It is a capability, and you can build it using tested guidance and routines, not hope and heroics (NIST, 2025a; NIST, 2025b).

Technology Is Not Strategy, It's an Amplifier

Technology amplifies what the organization already is. If you have clear roles, disciplined follow-through, and a culture where people report issues early, systems help you scale those strengths. If you have vague ownership, inconsistent expectations, and a habit of ignoring small problems, the same systems will mostly create noise, finger-pointing, and false reassurance.

This is why risk technology should be treated like any other control. It needs an owner. It needs performance measures. It needs periodic testing. It needs updates and governance. It needs a plan for when it fails. Too many organizations roll out a tool, celebrate adoption, and then slowly abandon it when reality does not fit the workflow. The tool becomes a "system we have," not a system we run.

If you want a fast test of whether a tool is helping, ask two questions:

- Can leadership use it to make a decision this month?
- Does it change behavior in the field in a way that reduces risk?

If the answer is no to both, you probably have activity, not progress.

The Risk Tech Stack: Systems That Quietly Run the Program

Risk management rarely lives in one platform. In most organizations, it's spread across a patchwork of systems that were purchased at different times for different reasons. That patchwork can still work, but only if the organization understands what each system is responsible for, and how information flows between them.

A typical risk tech ecosystem includes:

Risk and compliance systems (GRC). These track policies, controls, audits, risk registers, corrective actions, and sometimes vendor risk. Done well, they create accountability and a single record of truth. Done poorly, they become a place where risk goes to die in long forms and overdue tasks.

Safety and EHS systems. These support incident reporting, near-miss tracking, inspections, training records, and investigations. Their real value is not the reporting screen. It's whether they help you learn from patterns and close corrective actions in a way you can verify.

Claims and insurance systems. These hold loss data, reserves, payments, and claim classifications. They influence how leaders perceive the cost of risk and where resources get targeted.

Maintenance and asset systems (CMMS). These are risk systems, even if the organization doesn't call them that. Preventive maintenance completion and downtime trends are often leading indicators for injuries, breakdowns, and service failure.

HR and workforce systems. Staffing levels, turnover, overtime, and training compliance all sit here. System strain is often visible in HR data before it shows up as losses.

Security systems. Access control, camera systems, visitor management, and panic or duress systems can support safety, but they also carry privacy, labor, and data retention risks that need governance.

Cybersecurity monitoring and response tooling. If you have a Security Operations Center or a managed provider, you may have detection and response platforms. Even if you don't, you likely have endpoint protection, logging, and alerting somewhere. Those tools matter most when something goes wrong.

The risk leader's job is not to become the IT director. It is to understand how these systems affect risk decisions and control health. If the tech stack creates delays, conflicting data, or unclear ownership, it becomes a risk driver.

This is where standards help. ISO 45001 frames occupational health and safety as a management system with leadership, planning, support, operations, and continual improvement, which means technology should strengthen those loops, not sit outside them (ISO, 2018). In cybersecurity, ISO/IEC 27001 sets expectations for an information security management system, which includes risk treatment, controls, and continual improvement, not just tools (ISO, n.d.). And at the control catalog level, NIST SP 800-53 provides a structured way to think about security and privacy controls as part of risk management, not just technical configuration (NIST, 2020).

Sensors and Wearables: What They're Great At and What They Break

Sensors and wearables are attractive because they promise something risk leaders want badly: earlier warning. They can detect heat stress risk, fatigue signals, unsafe postures, near misses in vehicle operations, environmental exposures, equipment vibration patterns, and more. In some environments, they can absolutely reduce harm, especially when the hazard is predictable and the response action is clear.

But sensors also introduce three problems that risk leaders need to address upfront: false confidence, false alarms, and social fallout.

False confidence

A sensor can create the impression that risk is "covered" because the tool exists. But sensing is not controlling. It is monitoring. If the organization does not have a reliable response pathway, the sensor becomes a fancy way to collect evidence of inaction.

For example, an environmental sensor may detect air quality thresholds, but if the response requires shutting down work and no one has authority to do that, the organization will rationalize the alerts away. Now you have risk data that increases liability because it shows you knew.

False alarms and alert fatigue

Sensors rarely fail by being silent. They often fail by being too loud. If workers get constant alerts that do not match their lived experience, they learn to ignore them. The system may still be "working," but behavior changes in the wrong direction.

Risk leaders should demand basic performance questions during pilot phases: How often does the alert trigger? How often is it correct? What is the cost of a false positive? What is the cost of a missed event? These questions are as important as price.

Social fallout: privacy, trust, and compliance theater

Wearables and monitoring tools raise legitimate concerns about surveillance and fairness. If employees believe the tool will be used to discipline rather than protect, reporting drops and resistance rises. That resistance can be quiet, like non-use, or loud, like union pushback, grievances, and reputational damage.

A workable approach is to treat monitoring as a safety control with rules. Who can see individual data? When does data become part of an investigation? How long is it retained? How will it be used, and how will it not be used? If those questions cannot be answered in plain language, the tool is not ready.

The deeper point is that "people risk" is not separate from technology risk. Tools change behavior. Behavior changes outcomes. If the tool undermines trust, it may increase risk even if it improves measurement.

When Cyber Becomes Physical: Operational Technology and the Safety Connection

One reason technology has become central to risk management is that the boundary between cyber risk and physical risk is thinner than most leaders realize. It's one thing if a cyber incident takes down email. It's another if it disrupts building systems, fleet operations, manufacturing controls, water systems, emergency notification, security access controls, or any environment where digital compromise can affect physical outcomes.

This is where operational technology (OT) matters. OT environments include industrial control systems, supervisory control and data acquisition systems, and programmable logic controllers that run physical processes. NIST has long recognized that securing these systems requires a different mindset because performance, reliability, and safety requirements are unique (Stouffer et al., 2015). The ISA/IEC 62443 family similarly emphasizes a lifecycle approach to securing industrial automation and control systems, bridging IT and OT realities (ISA, n.d.).

For risk leaders, the practical implications are straightforward:

- A cyber event can shut down operations and create safety hazards through loss of control, loss of visibility, or forced workarounds.
- OT environments often have legacy equipment, limited patching windows, and vendor dependencies that complicate traditional IT security practices.
- If IT and operations teams do not coordinate, cyber controls can unintentionally create operational fragility, while operational priorities can unintentionally create cyber exposure.

A good governance move is to ensure cyber risk is represented in enterprise risk discussions, not as a technical "IT update," but as a business continuity and safety issue. NIST's Cybersecurity Framework 2.0 is useful here because it is built to help organizations manage cybersecurity as an enterprise risk, communicate priorities, and integrate governance, not just technical controls (NIST, 2024; NIST, 2024b).

The Cyber Side of Risk Management: Governance, Controls, and Zero Trust Reality

Cybersecurity becomes manageable when it is treated like risk management, not like a mystery. The organization needs a clear framework, control expectations, and decision pathways. Otherwise, cyber conversations become either panic-driven or overly technical, and leaders default to either denial or expensive shopping.

Two practical anchors are helpful:

A framework that leadership can understand

NIST CSF 2.0 gives organizations a way to understand, assess, prioritize, and communicate cybersecurity risk, and it elevates governance as a central element of the framework (NIST, 2024; NIST, 2024b). The value to risk leaders is not the diagram. The value is the shared language. It helps you connect cybersecurity to mission, operational resilience, and decision-making.

A control model that is testable

NIST SP 800-53 provides a catalog of security and privacy controls that can be tailored to the organization's environment and risk profile (NIST, 2020). ISO/IEC 27001 provides an ISMS structure, which is essentially a management system approach to information security, including risk treatment and continual improvement (ISO, n.d.). These tools help risk leaders move from "we have security tools" to "we have controls that are designed, implemented, monitored, and improved."

A concept that often shows up in cyber discussions is zero trust. The short version is that modern environments cannot rely on a trusted internal network boundary. NIST's guidance on zero trust architecture reflects this shift toward focusing on users, assets, and resources rather than assuming internal equals trusted (Rose et al., 2020). For risk leaders, zero trust is not something you buy. It is an approach that can reduce lateral movement risk and improve resilience when implemented thoughtfully.

The point is not to turn every risk manager into a cybersecurity architect. The point is to make sure the organization can answer basic governance questions:

- What are our most critical assets and services?
- What are our most likely threat paths?
- What controls matter most in our environment?
- How do we know those controls are operating?
- Who makes decisions during an incident?

If leadership cannot answer those questions, you do not have a cyber program. You have a set of tools.

Incident Response: The Difference Between a Plan and a Capability

Most organizations have an incident response plan. Fewer organizations have incident response capability. Capability shows up in speed, coordination, and decision quality under pressure. It shows up in whether people know who is in charge, how to escalate, how to communicate, and how to restore operations safely.

NIST's updated incident response guidance (SP 800-61 Rev. 3) explicitly connects incident response to cybersecurity risk management and governance, aiming to help organizations prepare, reduce impact, and improve detection and recovery (NIST, 2025a; NIST, 2025b). That framing matters because cyber incidents are not just technical events. They are operational and leadership events.

From a risk management perspective, incident response capability includes:

Decision roles and authority. Who can isolate systems? Who can shut down operations? Who can authorize external communications? If those roles are unclear, the organization will lose time and incur damage.

Communication discipline. Internal messages need to be consistent and accurate, and external messages must be truthful and coordinated. Conflicting statements create reputational harm and legal exposure.

Continuity and recovery. Restoring systems is not just about turning things back on. It's about restoring safely. Workarounds can create hazards if they bypass controls.

Learning and improvement. After-action reviews should result in actual changes to controls, training, and governance. Otherwise, you repeat the incident with better slides.

A practical sign of maturity is whether the organization runs realistic exercises, not just check-the-box tabletop sessions. Realistic means testing the messy parts: communications, decision authority, vendor responsiveness, and what happens at 2:00 a.m. when the right person is not reachable.

When Tools Hurt: Automation Bias, Vendor Risk, and the "Dashboard Lie"

Technology can degrade risk management in ways that are easy to miss until the moment it matters.

Automation bias

Automation bias is when people over-trust outputs because they came from a system. In risk work, that looks like ignoring frontline signals because the dashboard is green, or delaying action because a model did not flag the risk.

The danger is not that analytics is wrong. The danger is that analytics becomes the only voice in the room. Risk leaders should actively protect "human sensing" alongside technical sensing, especially in high-stakes environments where weak signals matter.

Vendor and supply chain risk

Many risk tools are cloud-based and vendor-supported. That adds dependencies. If the vendor goes down, you may lose access to incident reports, inspection schedules, training records, or security monitoring. Vendor performance and contractual expectations become part of your risk posture.

Cybersecurity frameworks and control catalogs emphasize supply chain and third-party considerations for a reason. If your critical controls are outsourced, you need clear service expectations, audit rights, and incident reporting requirements.

The dashboard lie

Dashboards can lie without anyone intending to lie. They lie when definitions are inconsistent. They lie when exposure is ignored. They lie when underreporting is rewarded. They lie when the metrics reflect activity rather than control effectiveness. You can have perfect visualization of bad data.

The corrective move is boring but powerful: tighten definitions, validate inputs, and tie metrics to decisions and verification. Technology works best when paired with governance.

Selecting and Implementing Risk Technology Without Regretting It Later

Most tech failures are not technical. They are adoption failures, governance failures, and expectation failures.

A sane implementation approach is built around a few moves:

Start with the decision you're trying to improve, not the feature list.
Pilot in one area where leadership is engaged and follow-through is real.
Build simple workflows first, then expand. Complexity early kills adoption.

Define ownership clearly. If no one owns corrective actions, they will age out and become noise.

Train for competence, not attendance. A tool is only as good as the people using it. Measure whether the tool changed outcomes or control health. If it didn't, adjust or stop.

Risk leaders should also insist on an exit plan. If the vendor relationship ends or the tool fails, how do you retain access to records and continue critical functions? This sounds pessimistic until a crisis happens and no one can log in.

Finally, treat cybersecurity as part of procurement. A tool that introduces weak security practices can increase risk while claiming to reduce it. Frameworks like NIST CSF and control catalogs like NIST SP 800-53 help set expectations and evaluate posture (NIST, 2024; NIST, 2020).

Closing

Technology can be one of the strongest allies risk management has, but only when the organization uses it with discipline. Systems can create clarity, speed, and accountability. Sensors can provide early warnings that prevent injuries and failures. Cyber controls and incident response can keep operations stable when threats hit. At the same time, tools can create new hazards through overconfidence, backlash against surveillance, vendor dependence, and misleading metrics.

A grounded way to lead here is to treat technology like any other risk decision. Ask what it changes, what it introduces, and what it requires from people to work well. Pair tools with governance. Protect trust. Build response capability, not just documentation. If you do that, technology becomes what it should be: a support for safer work, better decisions, and resilience when things get real.

References

International Organization for Standardization. (2018). *ISO 45001:2018 Occupational health and safety management systems—Requirements with guidance for use*. ISO.

International Organization for Standardization. (n.d.). *ISO/IEC 27001:2022 Information security management systems*. ISO.

International Society of Automation. (n.d.). *ISA/IEC 62443 series of standards*. ISA.

National Institute of Standards and Technology. (2020). *Security and privacy controls for information systems and organizations (SP 800-53 Rev. 5)*. NIST.

National Institute of Standards and Technology. (2024). *The NIST Cybersecurity Framework (CSF) 2.0 (NIST CSWP 29)*. NIST.

National Institute of Standards and Technology. (2025a). *Incident response recommendations and considerations for cybersecurity risk management (SP 800-61 Rev. 3)*. NIST.

National Institute of Standards and Technology. (2025b). *NIST revises SP 800-61: Incident response recommendations and considerations for cybersecurity risk management* (announcement). NIST.

Rose, S., Borchert, O., Mitchell, S., & Connelly, S. (2020). *Zero trust architecture (SP 800-207)*. NIST.

Stouffer, K., Pillitteri, V., Lightman, S., Abrams, M., & Hahn, A. (2015). *Guide to industrial control systems (ICS) security (SP 800-82 Rev. 2)*. NIST.

Chapter 13
AI and Cognitive Technologies in Risk Management

Smarter tools, same accountability

AI and Cognitive Technologies in Risk Management: Smarter tools, same accountability

AI has become the new intern who never sleeps. It reads faster than we do, flags patterns we would miss, and drafts clean summaries when we are buried in emails and incident reports. It also shows up with the same problems every "perfect" assistant brings: it can be confidently wrong, it can miss context, and it can quietly shift how people make decisions without anyone noticing the shift until something goes sideways. If you lead risk, the question is not whether AI is coming. It is already here. The real question is whether you will use it as a disciplined tool that strengthens judgment, or let it become a glossy shortcut that weakens accountability (NIST, 2023; NIST, 2024a).

Key learnings, in plain language: AI in risk management is not magic, it is pattern recognition and language processing at scale, applied to real operational decisions. It can improve speed, consistency, and early warning, especially in claims, safety, compliance, fraud, and cyber. The trade-off is that AI introduces new failure modes, such as bias, automation bias, privacy leakage, model attacks, and model drift, which slowly erodes performance over time (Parasuraman & Riley, 1997; Skitka, Mosier, & Burdick, 1999; NIST, 2024a). Frameworks like the NIST AI Risk Management Framework and ISO and IEC's AI management system standard can help you build governance that is practical instead of theoretical (NIST, 2023; International Organization for Standardization & International Electrotechnical Commission, 2023). And no matter how advanced the tool becomes, the responsibility stays with people. You can delegate tasks to systems, but you cannot delegate accountability.

What we mean by AI and cognitive technologies in a risk shop

Much of the confusion starts with vocabulary. In risk management, "AI" is usually a bundle of capabilities that range from traditional predictive models to modern generative tools. Some of it is quietly embedded in systems you already use. Some of it is new, exciting, and a little unstable.

Most of what shows up in risk work falls into a few practical buckets:

Machine learning models that score or predict. These are the tools that estimate severity, prioritize workload, or flag anomalies. They are often used for claims triage, fraud detection, or safety trend prediction. They can be powerful, but they require ongoing validation and monitoring, much like any other decision model you would defend in front of an auditor, regulator, or court (Federal Reserve Board, 2011).

Natural language processing tools that read and summarize. These systems can scan adjuster notes, medical narratives, grievance records, emails, inspection writeups, policies, and contracts. They reduce administrative drag and help teams find the needle in the haystack. They also raise questions about confidentiality and retention, especially when sensitive data is involved (NIST, 2024a).

Computer vision systems that interpret images and video. Think dashcam footage, jobsite cameras, facility access control, and certain inspection workflows. These can support safety coaching and investigations, but they also bring privacy concerns and, in some cases, heightened legal exposure if the technology is used for employee monitoring without clear boundaries (UNESCO, 2021).

Generative AI systems that draft, explain, and simulate. These tools can produce summaries, draft communications, generate training scenarios, and help teams explore "what if" conditions. They can also hallucinate, meaning they generate plausible-sounding content that is not true, and they can inadvertently reveal sensitive information if used carelessly (NIST, 2024a; OWASP, 2024).

"Cognitive technologies" is a useful umbrella term when multiple techniques are combined into something that feels like reasoning. In practice, that usually means a workflow that blends rules, models, retrieval from internal documents, and human review into a decision support loop. The important distinction is not what vendors call it. The important distinction is how it is used.

There are two basic modes: automation and augmentation. Automation replaces a human step. Augmentation supports human decisions. In low-stakes workflows, automation can be fine. In high-stakes workflows, especially those that affect employment, discipline, eligibility, student outcomes, patient outcomes, or public benefits, augmentation is usually the safer lane. It keeps humans responsible for the final decision and reduces the temptation to treat a score as truth (Parasuraman & Riley, 1997; Skitka et al., 1999).

Where AI is already changing risk management work

For most organizations, the best starting point is not "How do we buy AI?" It is "Where are we already using it without naming it?" When you answer that honestly, you usually find AI in at least four areas: claims, safety, compliance, and cyber.

In claims and workers' compensation, AI is commonly used to triage, predict severity, detect fraud signals, and summarize documents. This can be genuinely helpful. It can route complex files to experienced adjusters early, reduce cycle time, and highlight patterns that suggest a claim needs closer review. The risk is just as real: a model can become a black box that influences claim handling without transparency, and that can become a problem when someone asks, "Why was this claim treated differently?" (Federal Reserve Board, 2011; NIST, 2023).

In safety, AI often appears through telematics, wearables, predictive maintenance analytics, and video analysis. Used well, it can support coaching, spot leading indicators, and shift safety from reactive to preventive. Used poorly, it turns into surveillance culture and "gotcha" management, which crushes reporting and trust. Risk leaders have to watch that line carefully because safety culture is fragile. People change what they report when they feel watched.

In compliance and governance, AI is increasingly used to search policies, draft control narratives, summarize audits, and detect exceptions in large datasets. It can reduce busywork, but it also creates a new dependence: people stop reading the original sources and start trusting the summary. That is not a small issue. If your compliance posture depends on summaries that can be wrong, you have created a quiet vulnerability.

In cybersecurity, AI is both a defense and an attack surface. It can help detect anomalies, triage alerts, and support incident response. It also introduces new risks: model theft, data poisoning, prompt injection, and supply chain vulnerabilities that did not exist in older software patterns (NIST, 2019; MITRE, n.d.; OWASP, 2024). If you treat AI systems like ordinary software, you will miss important threats.

The risks that matter: bias, drift, over-trust, privacy, and security

Most risk leaders do not need a lecture on "AI ethics." They need a clear view of how these systems fail in the real world, and what those failures mean operationally.

Bias is not theoretical. It shows up when models learn patterns from historical data that reflect unequal access, unequal treatment, or unequal reporting. A well-known example comes from healthcare, where an algorithm widely used to identify patients for care management underestimated the needs of Black patients because it used healthcare cost as a proxy for illness burden. Lower cost did not mean lower need. It meant different access and spending patterns (Obermeyer et al., 2019). Risk leaders should read that as a general lesson: if the proxy is flawed, the outputs will be flawed, even if the model is "accurate" by narrow technical metrics.

Model drift is a slow-erosion problem. Claims patterns change. Injury reporting changes. Workforces shift. Vendors change forms and coding. Regulations change incentives. A model that performed well last year can quietly become less reliable this year. Drift is why governance must include monitoring, thresholds, and retraining rules, not just an approval memo at implementation (NIST, 2023).

Automation bias is the human side of the equation. People tend to over-trust automated recommendations, especially under time pressure. Research in human factors has documented how decision aids can increase errors when people defer to the system instead of checking it (Parasuraman & Riley, 1997; Skitka et al., 1999). This is not solved by telling staff "be careful." It is addressed by designing the workflow so humans must engage, making the rationale visible where possible, and building accountability into how recommendations are used (Skitka, 2000).

Privacy and confidentiality risks are amplified by generative tools. If employees paste claim notes, student records, medical details, or investigation summaries into a public or unmanaged AI tool, you can create a record you did not intend to create and a disclosure you did not intend to make. Even when tools are internal, you need clear policies on what data can be used, how it is retained, and how access is controlled (NIST, 2024a; UNESCO, 2021).

Security is now part of the AI conversation, not separate from it. Models can be attacked. Training data can be poisoned. Systems can be manipulated through prompt injection. Outputs can be used as a pathway for social engineering. Threat modeling for AI needs to be a normal part of implementation, not an optional add-on after deployment (NIST, 2019; MITRE, n.d.; OWASP, 2024).

Governance you can defend: NIST AI RMF, ISO, and IEC, and the direction of regulation

A common mistake is to build AI governance as a separate project that sits outside the existing risk program. The better approach is to treat AI as any other enterprise capability that affects decision-making and then adapt your current governance structure to address the differences.

The NIST AI Risk Management Framework is useful because it is written in risk language rather than vendor language. It organizes the work into four functions: Govern, Map, Measure, and Manage (NIST, 2023). That structure fits how risk leaders already think. Governance is not just about policies. It is ownership, decision rights, documentation, and escalation paths. Mapping is understanding the system context, the stakeholders affected, the data sources, and the intended use. Measuring is testing performance, reliability, fairness concerns, and resilience. Managing is putting controls in place and monitoring the system over time.

NIST also published a Generative AI profile as a companion to the framework, which is invaluable because it calls out risks unique to or amplified by generative tools, such as hallucinations, data leakage, prompt injection, and content-provenance challenges (NIST, 2024a). If your organization is experimenting with AI copilots, chatbots, summarizers, or auto-drafting tools, this profile provides practical categories of risk to address.

ISO and IEC's ISO/IEC 42001 standard is also worth attention because it frames AI governance as a management system, not a one-time compliance task. It aligns with the logic that many organizations already know from ISO-style systems: define scope, assign roles, document processes, implement controls, audit, and improve (International Organization for Standardization & International Electrotechnical Commission, 2023). For risk leaders, the value is simple: it gives you a structure to say, "This is how we govern AI like we govern safety, security, or quality."

Regulation is moving in the same direction: risk-based requirements, documentation, monitoring, and accountability. The EU AI Act, for example, sets out obligations for "high risk" AI systems and includes expectations around a risk management system across the lifecycle (European Parliament and Council of the European Union, 2024; European Commission, 2024). Even if you are not in Europe, the direction matters because vendors and multinational partners will increasingly adopt these practices as default, and because many organizations want governance that will hold up across jurisdictions.

The strongest governance posture is not "we complied with the minimum." It is "we can explain how the system works, how it was tested, how it is monitored, and who is accountable when it fails." That posture travels well.

A practical AI game plan for risk leaders

Risk leaders do not need a 60-page AI strategy document to start. They need a clear sequence and a few rules that prevent predictable mistakes.

Start with an inventory. List every tool that uses predictive scoring, anomaly detection, natural language summarization, or automated recommendations. Include vendor tools, internal scripts, and anything a department is using informally. If you cannot name it, you cannot govern it. This is the same logic as asset management in cybersecurity. Unknown systems become unmanaged systems.

Next, classify use cases by stakes. A model that prioritizes which inspection to schedule first is not the same as a model that influences discipline, hiring, student placement, or benefit decisions. High-stakes use cases warrant stronger controls: more rigorous validation, clearer documentation, tighter monitoring, and explicit human decision-making responsibility (NIST, 2023; OECD, 2019).

Then define what "acceptable" looks like. Accuracy is not enough. You need performance thresholds, drift indicators, and a standard approach for explaining recommendations to users. If the model is not explainable in a technical sense, you still need operational explainability: what inputs matter, what limitations exist, when not to use the output, and what escalation looks like (NIST, 2023).

Build in human checks where they matter most. If an AI tool recommends an action that impacts a person's livelihood, benefits, education, or safety, you want a workflow that forces review. Not a rubber stamp. A real review with responsibility attached. This is where lessons from automation bias matter. People defer to systems when the system feels authoritative and the human feels rushed (Parasuraman & Riley, 1997; Skitka et al., 1999).

Treat AI like software from a security standpoint, and then go further. Use secure development practices and vendor security requirements. Evaluate data access, logging, and retention. Threat model the AI-specific risks, including prompt injection and data poisoning. If you are deploying generative tools, follow known risk patterns from the AI security community and make it part of your baseline controls (NIST, 2019; NIST, 2022; OWASP, 2024).

Finally, make the success measures concrete. In claims, that could be reduced cycle time without increased dispute rates. In safety, that could result in fewer high-severity incidents without reduced reporting volume. In compliance, that could be faster audit preparation without increased corrections after review. If the metric is only "we used AI," you are not managing risk. You are collecting gadgets.

Conclusion: smarter tools, same accountability

AI can make risk management sharper. It can reduce noise, improve prioritization, and help teams act earlier instead of later. But it will not save an organization from weak leadership, unclear accountability, or a culture that avoids hard conversations. Those are human issues, and they stay human issues no matter how advanced the tools become.

If you remember one thing from this chapter, let it be this: the right question is rarely "Can AI do this?" The right question is "Should we use AI here, and if we do, can we explain it, monitor it, and own the outcome?" When the answer is yes, AI can be a real advantage. When the answer is no, the most responsible move is to slow down, redesign the use case, or keep the decision where it belongs, with informed people who are willing to be accountable.

References

European Commission. (2024). *AI Act Service Desk: Article 9 risk management system.*

European Parliament and Council of the European Union. (2024). *Regulation (EU) 2024/1689 of the European Parliament and of the Council of 13 June 2024 laying down harmonised rules on artificial intelligence (Artificial Intelligence Act).*

Federal Reserve Board. (2011). *SR 11-7: Guidance on model risk management.*

International Organization for Standardization, & International Electrotechnical Commission. (2023). *ISO/IEC 42001:2023 Artificial intelligence management system requirements.*

MITRE. (n.d.). *ATLAS: Adversarial Threat Landscape for Artificial-Intelligence Systems.*

National Institute of Standards and Technology. (2019). *A taxonomy and terminology of adversarial machine learning.* U.S. Department of Commerce.

National Institute of Standards and Technology. (2022). *NIST AI RMF Playbook.* U.S. Department of Commerce.

National Institute of Standards and Technology. (2023). *Artificial Intelligence Risk Management Framework (AI RMF 1.0).* U.S. Department of Commerce.

National Institute of Standards and Technology. (2024a). *Artificial Intelligence Risk Management Framework: Generative Artificial Intelligence Profile (NIST AI 600-1).* U.S. Department of Commerce.

OECD. (2019). *Recommendation of the Council on Artificial Intelligence.*

Obermeyer, Z., Powers, B., Vogeli, C., & Mullainathan, S. (2019). Dissecting racial bias in an algorithm used to manage the health of populations. *Science, 366*(6464), 447–453.

OWASP. (2024). *Top 10 for Large Language Model Applications (2023–2024).*

Parasuraman, R., & Riley, V. (1997). Humans and automation: Use, misuse, disuse, abuse. *Human Factors, 39*(2), 230–253.

Skitka, L. J., Mosier, K. L., & Burdick, M. (1999). Does automation bias decision-making? *International Journal of Human-Computer Studies, 51*(5), 991–1006.

Skitka, L. J. (2000). Accountability and automation bias. *International Journal of Human-Computer Studies, 52*(4), 701–717.

UNESCO. (2021). *Recommendation on the ethics of artificial intelligence.*

Chapter 14
Behavioral Economics and Risk Decisions

Why smart people still make risky choices

Why smart people still make risky choices

If risk were only a logic problem, most organizations would be safer than they are. The policies would be read, the training would stick, the near misses would be reported, and the same claims wouldn't keep showing up year after year with slightly different names attached. But risk is not just a technical issue. It's human behavior under pressure, under incentives, and under imperfect information. That's why you can put brilliant people in a room, give them the same facts, and still watch them make decisions that look irrational in hindsight.

Behavioral economics helps explain what's really happening. Not because people are "dumb," but because the brain is built for speed, social belonging, and survival, not for perfect statistical reasoning (Kahneman, 2011). We rely on shortcuts. We misread probabilities. We avoid losses more aggressively than we chase gains. We tell ourselves stories that make our choices feel reasonable. And in organizations, those individual tendencies get amplified by culture, hierarchy, deadlines, and the quiet pressure to keep things moving.

The central learnings of this chapter are simple to say and harder to live. Risk decisions are shaped as much by framing, incentives, and emotion as they are by data, and that means the "best" technical solution can fail if it ignores human behavior (Tversky & Kahneman, 1981; Thaler & Sunstein, 2008). Most preventable losses are not caused by a lack of knowledge, but by predictable patterns like overconfidence, normalization of deviance, short-term thinking, and social proof, especially when people are tired, rushed, or trying to avoid conflict (Kahneman & Tversky, 1979; Ariely, 2008; Cialdini, 2009). Finally, the strongest risk leaders do not try to "train bias out of people." They design decisions, environments, and systems that make safer choices easier and risky shortcuts harder, while preserving dignity and accountability (Thaler & Sunstein, 2008; Bazerman & Moore, 2013).

The myth of the rational decision-maker

Classic economics often assumes people make decisions like calculators: clear preferences, consistent choices, and rational tradeoffs. Real life doesn't work that way, and anyone who has worked in claims, safety, HR, operations, or cyber knows it. People are inconsistent. They take shortcuts. They avoid discomfort. They follow the crowd. They pick the option that feels simplest, even when it's not the safest.

Herbert Simon called this "bounded rationality." People do not optimize. They "satisfice." They make a decision that feels good enough given limited time, limited attention, and limited information (Simon, 1955). That idea is a relief, honestly. It explains why smart, well-meaning people still cut corners. They're not necessarily choosing harm. They're choosing relief: relief from friction, time pressure, social tension, or cognitive load.

Kahneman's "System 1 and System 2" framing adds another layer. System 1 is fast, intuitive, and automatic. System 2 is slower, effortful, and analytical (Kahneman, 2011). System 1 runs most of the day. System 2 shows up when something forces it to. Risk often lives in the space where System 1 is making speed-based decisions in environments that actually require System 2 thinking.

This is why simply telling people "be careful" rarely works. It assumes people are choosing risk thoughtfully. Many risky choices happen because people are trying to move, trying to keep pace, trying to avoid trouble, or trying to meet expectations. If you want better decisions, you have to understand the behavioral forces shaping them.

Prospect theory and the hidden power of loss aversion

One of the most important insights in behavioral economics is prospect theory: people experience losses more intensely than equivalent gains (Kahneman & Tversky, 1979). Losing $100 hurts more than gaining $100 feels good. That simple fact drives a shocking amount of organizational behavior.

Loss aversion shows up in risk management in ways that are easy to miss:

- A department resists a safety change not because it's unsafe, but because it feels like a loss of autonomy.
- Leaders delay a needed shutdown because it feels like a loss of productivity, even if it prevents a larger loss later.
- A manager avoids reporting a near miss because it feels like a loss of reputation or control.
- An organization keeps an aging system running because replacing it feels like an upfront loss, even if the long-term risk is higher.

Loss aversion also explains why corrective actions often stall. Corrective action requires someone to admit something was wrong, or incomplete, or neglected. That admission feels like a loss. So the organization negotiates with reality instead. It re-labels the problem. It downplays severity. It asks for "more information." Weeks pass. Then the incident happens again, and now the loss is real.

Prospect theory also introduced the idea that people evaluate outcomes relative to a reference point, not in absolute terms (Kahneman & Tversky, 1979). In organizations, the reference point is often "normal operations." Anything that disrupts normal operations is felt as a loss, even if it's necessary. That's why resilience and prevention investments face such resistance. You're asking people to absorb pain now to avoid pain later, and human psychology is not naturally built for that.

Framing: the same facts, different decisions

Tversky and Kahneman showed that how a choice is framed can dramatically change decisions, even when the underlying outcomes are identical (Tversky & Kahneman, 1981). In risk management, framing is one of the most powerful tools leaders either use intentionally or stumble into accidentally.

Consider two ways to present the same safety investment:

"Spending $250,000 to improve controls."
"Preventing one severe injury and two lost-time cases a year, reducing downtime, and protecting service continuity."

Both can be true. But the second frame connects to mission, human impact, and operational stability. The first frame triggers a cost reflex. When leaders frame risk only as cost, they unintentionally set up prevention as optional. When leaders frame prevention as continuity, reliability, and defensible leadership, they create a different decision atmosphere.

Framing also matters in claims discussions. If a claims trend is framed as "employees are getting hurt more," it can become a blame conversation. If it's framed as "these tasks and conditions are producing predictable injuries," it becomes a systems conversation. The data might be the same, but the moral temperature changes, and that changes decisions.

Risk leaders need to be careful here. Framing is not manipulation. It's clarity. The ethical version of framing is presenting the full truth in a way that connects to what people value and understand.

Overconfidence and optimism bias: "It won't happen here"

Overconfidence is not a character flaw. It's a cognitive default. Most people overestimate their ability, underestimate uncertainty, and assume the future will resemble the recent past (Kahneman, 2011). In risk management, this shows up as optimism bias: "We're different," "We're careful," "We've never had that happen," or the classic, "That's a big-city problem."

Optimism bias is especially dangerous in low-frequency, high-severity risks: workplace violence, catastrophic injuries, major cyber incidents, facility fires, major equipment failures, and reputational crises. When the event is rare, the absence of evidence gets mistaken for evidence of absence. People interpret "nothing happened" as "we are safe," instead of "we got lucky."

Overconfidence also drives poor incident investigation. A leader might assume they already know the cause. They look for evidence that confirms it. They stop listening. Confirmation bias locks in the first story that feels right (Nickerson, 1998). Meanwhile, the real causes stay in the shadows: staffing strain, equipment downtime, workarounds, unclear procedures, supervision gaps, or incentive pressures.

The fix is not to shame leaders for being human. The fix is to build decision processes that force humility. Premortems are one example: before implementing a decision, you imagine it failed and ask why (Klein, 2007). That technique creates permission to surface risks without sounding negative.

Present bias and short-termism: tomorrow's risk loses to today's pain

Present bias is the tendency to overweight immediate costs and underweight future benefits. In behavioral economics, this is closely linked to time inconsistency and hyperbolic discounting (Laibson, 1997). In plain terms, people say they want long-term safety and resilience, but when the short-term pain arrives, they choose the option that feels easier right now.

This is why:

- Preventive maintenance gets delayed until it becomes emergency maintenance.
- Training becomes a checkbox because competency takes time.
- Safety observations become "quick drive-bys" because deeper coaching takes effort.

- Cyber patching gets postponed because downtime is inconvenient.
  Resilience planning gets pushed off because "we have more urgent priorities."

Organizations don't usually do this because they hate safety. They do it because incentives and pressures reward short-term output. Leaders who want better risk outcomes have to confront this honestly. If the organization praises speed and punishes delay, people will take shortcuts. If the organization celebrates "getting it done" more than "getting it right," controls will degrade.

Behavioral economics doesn't just diagnose this. It gives a direction for solutions: change defaults, reduce friction for the right choices, and make long-term benefits visible in the short-term story (Thaler & Sunstein, 2008).

Social norms and the power of "how we do things here"

Many risky decisions are not "decisions" at all. They're norms. People do what is normal around them. Cialdini's research on social influence describes how strongly people follow descriptive norms, meaning what they perceive others are doing (Cialdini, 2009). In a workplace, descriptive norms can beat formal policy every time.

If the norm is to report near misses, people report. If the norm is to hide mistakes, people hide. If the norm is to "handle it quietly," incidents disappear from the system until they become lawsuits. If the norm is to joke about safety rules, the rules become optional.

This is why culture is not a soft concept in risk management. Culture is a control environment. It shapes what people pay attention to, what they feel safe saying, and what they believe will happen if they speak up. When the norm is silence, leadership loses early warning, and risk becomes reactive.

A practical point: social norms are not changed by posters. They are changed by what leaders reward and what leaders tolerate. If a supervisor dismisses reporting, that becomes the rule. If a leader responds to reporting with learning and action, that becomes the rule.

Scarcity, stress, and cognitive load: the risk multiplier nobody budgets for

The most dangerous decisions often happen when people are tired, rushed, understaffed, or overloaded. Scarcity and stress narrow attention. People focus on immediate tasks and miss broader risks. This is not a moral failure. It's a predictable human response.

Behavioral research on scarcity suggests that when people experience scarcity, whether time, money, or bandwidth, it captures attention and reduces cognitive resources for other decisions (Mullainathan & Shafir, 2013). In organizations, that means staffing shortages, overtime, and constant urgency can quietly degrade risk performance even when people are trying hard.

You can see it in claims patterns: more strains, more slips, more vehicle incidents, more errors. You can see it in compliance: missed steps, incomplete documentation, rushed investigations. You can see it in cyber: delayed patches, weak passwords, bypassed controls because "we just need access now."

If you want a serious risk program, you have to treat workload and staffing as risk drivers, not just HR issues. You can't preach safe behavior into an exhausted workforce.

Normalization of deviance: how "temporary workarounds" become permanent risk

Some of the costliest risk decisions start as small compromises. A procedure is inconvenient, so someone skips a step "just this once." Nothing bad happens. The shortcut becomes easier. The shortcut becomes normal. Over time, the organization stops seeing it as a shortcut and begins to view it as the real procedure.

This pattern is often described as normalization of deviance, the gradual acceptance of practices that drift away from standards because negative outcomes don't immediately occur. Diane Vaughan's work on the Challenger disaster is a landmark example of how organizations can normalize signals of danger over time, especially under pressure to perform (Vaughan, 1996).

In everyday risk management, normalization looks like this:

- Equipment used without guards because guards slow production.
- Ladders used when lifts should be used, because it's "faster."
- Lockout steps shortened because "we've done it this way for years."
- Incident reports minimized because "it was nothing."
- Access controls bypassed because "IT takes too long."

The fix is partly technical and partly cultural. You need controls that make the safe path workable, and you need leadership that refuses to treat deviation as normal. You also need learning systems that capture small deviations before they become disasters.

Behavioral solutions that actually work in organizations

Here's where behavioral economics earns its keep. It's not just a critique of human decision-making. It offers practical design principles.

Choice architecture: make the safe choice the easy choice

Thaler and Sunstein popularized the idea of "choice architecture," meaning the way choices are structured influences decisions (Thaler & Sunstein, 2008). In risk management, this is a gold mine.

- If you want higher reporting, make reporting easy, fast, and psychologically safe.
- If you want preventive maintenance completed, design workflows and scheduling that don't punish managers for downtime.
- If you want training to matter, build competency checks into the process rather than relying on attendance.
- If you want better cyber behavior, reduce password friction and implement safer defaults rather than blaming users.

Defaults matter. People tend to stick with defaults because changing them requires effort and attention. So set defaults that protect safety and security and require conscious choice to override them.

Add friction to risky shortcuts

Organizations are good at adding friction to safe behavior. They make reporting hard. They make procurement slow. They make approvals unclear. Then they wonder why people work around the system.

Behavioral design flips that. If a shortcut is risky, add small friction to slow it down. Require a second set of eyes for high-risk decisions. Require a quick risk check before approving a deviation. Require a documented rationale for overrides. The goal is not bureaucracy. The goal is to force a pause where System 2 thinking can show up.

Use premortems and red teams to fight overconfidence

Premortems reduce optimism bias by making risk discussion legitimate before failure occurs (Klein, 2007). Red teams do something similar by assigning a group to challenge assumptions and look for failure paths. In risk governance, these tools protect against groupthink and help leaders see blind spots earlier.

Improve feedback loops so people can learn

People adjust their behavior when they see consequences and learn quickly. Risk systems often fail because feedback is delayed or invisible. Someone reports a hazard, and nothing happens. They stop reporting. Someone does safety observations, and no one closes actions. They stop caring. Behavioral economics reinforces a basic truth: behavior follows reinforcement.

So close loops. Communicate actions taken. Show trends. Share "what changed because you reported." This is not PR. It is behavioral reinforcement.

Treat incentives like risk controls

If bonus structures reward speed and punish downtime, you will get shortcuts. If performance reviews focus on output but ignore control health, you will get drift. People respond to incentives even when they don't want to admit it.

This is where risk leaders need courage. They need to ask: what behaviors does our system reward, and what risks does that create? Then they need to propose changes that align incentives with prevention and resilience.

Decision hygiene: the habits of organizations that make better risk choices

The most resilient organizations don't rely on hope. They rely on habits. A few habits show up again and again:

- They separate data from blame. They investigate systems, not just individuals.
- They use structured decision reviews for high-stakes choices, including assumptions and alternatives.
- They encourage dissent and protect people who surface concerns.
- They track leading indicators of control health, not just lagging outcomes.
- They learn visibly. They revise processes after incidents, and they check whether the revision worked.

These habits can sound like culture talk, but they're operational. They are how organizations reduce the effect of predictable human bias without pretending humans will stop being human.

Closing

Smart people make risky choices for predictable reasons. They are influenced by framing, loss aversion, time pressure, social norms, stress, and incentives that push toward short-term relief. Behavioral economics gives risk leaders something valuable: a way to stop moralizing and start designing. The goal is not to eliminate judgment. The goal is to support sound judgment by making it easier to make safe, ethical, defensible choices, even on hard days.

If you want a simple reflection to carry forward, ask this: where do we keep expecting willpower to beat design? Wherever the answer is "often," you have a risk opportunity. Redesign the choice. Change the default. Improve the feedback loop. Add a pause where it matters. And make sure the organization's incentives do not quietly reward the very shortcuts you're trying to eliminate.

References

Ariely, D. (2008). *Predictably irrational: The hidden forces that shape our decisions.* HarperCollins.

Bazerman, M. H., & Moore, D. A. (2013). *Judgment in managerial decision making* (8th ed.). Wiley.

Cialdini, R. B. (2009). *Influence: Science and practice* (5th ed.). Pearson.

Kahneman, D. (2011). *Thinking, fast and slow.* Farrar, Straus and Giroux.

Kahneman, D., & Tversky, A. (1979). Prospect theory: An analysis of decision under risk. *Econometrica, 47*(2), 263–291.

Klein, G. (2007). Performing a project premortem. *Harvard Business Review, 85*(9), 18–19.

Laibson, D. (1997). Golden eggs and hyperbolic discounting. *Quarterly Journal of Economics, 112*(2), 443–477.

Mullainathan, S., & Shafir, E. (2013). *Scarcity: Why having too little means so much.* Times Books.

Nickerson, R. S. (1998). Confirmation bias: A ubiquitous phenomenon in many guises. *Review of General Psychology, 2*(2), 175–220.

Simon, H. A. (1955). A behavioral model of rational choice. *Quarterly Journal of Economics, 69*(1), 99–118.

Thaler, R. H., & Sunstein, C. R. (2008). *Nudge: Improving decisions about health, wealth, and happiness.* Yale University Press.

Tversky, A., & Kahneman, D. (1981). The framing of decisions and the psychology of choice. *Science, 211*(4481), 453–458.

Vaughan, D. (1996). *The Challenger launch decision: Risky technology, culture, and deviance at NASA.* University of Chicago Press.

Part: V – Strategy, Sustainability, Global Risk

Chapter 15
Sustainability, ESG, and Risk

Why long-term thinking is now a risk requirement

Why long-term thinking is now a risk requirement

Many leaders still talk about sustainability as if it were a values statement or a branding choice. Something you do if you have the time, the budget, or the "right kind" of customers. That framing is outdated. Sustainability is now a risk conversation because the underlying drivers are no longer theoretical. Heat, wildfire, flood, water stress, supply disruptions, regulatory swings, talent expectations, litigation risk, and insurance market behavior are showing up in operating costs and continuity decisions. The question has shifted from "Do we care?" to "Can we defend our choices when the long-term becomes the short-term?"

The ESG label has not helped. It got politicized. It got packaged as a score. It got sold as a shortcut. And in some organizations, it became a slide deck that lived outside the risk program. Meanwhile, the risk signals kept getting louder. Climate-related physical risks and transition risks are now part of strategic, operational, financial, and reputational risks, whether an organization uses the term ESG or not (IPCC, 2023). So the practical stance for risk leaders is simple: stop treating sustainability as a separate initiative and start treating it like any other material risk domain that requires governance, data, controls, and decision discipline.

One reason this matters right now is that the rules are changing in uneven ways across jurisdictions. In the United States, the SEC voted in March 2025 to end the defense of its climate disclosure rules, a major shift in posture after the rules were adopted in 2024 and then stayed amid litigation (SEC, 2025). In Europe, the Corporate Sustainability Reporting Directive was designed to expand reporting obligations, but late 2025 saw political momentum to scale back parts of the EU's corporate sustainability requirements, with reporting thresholds and timelines being debated and revised heading into 2026 (European Commission, n.d.; Reuters, 2025a; Reuters, 2025b). In California, climate disclosure laws have faced legal challenges and injunctions, and the compliance outlook has become a moving target even as companies and investors continue to demand comparable data (The Wall Street Journal, 2025). In other words, the compliance map is real, but it is not stable, and that instability itself is a risk input.

The main learnings of this chapter can be stated plainly. First, sustainability risk is now a governance issue, not a communications issue, and it belongs inside the enterprise risk framework (ISO, 2018; COSO, 2017). Second, ESG reporting is increasingly about data quality and defensibility because markets and regulators are converging on disclosure frameworks even as politics diverges (IFRS Foundation, 2023a; IFRS Foundation, 2023b).

Third, long-term thinking is not a moral upgrade. It is a practical requirement for resilience because the most expensive losses are often those that were "unlikely" until they weren't (IPCC, 2023).

What sustainability risk actually is

Sustainability risk is often misunderstood because it gets reduced to carbon and recycling. Real sustainability risk is broader. It's any material risk tied to environmental limits, social stability, and governance integrity that can affect an organization's ability to achieve objectives over time. That includes climate, energy volatility, water, biodiversity and nature dependencies, labor conditions in supply chains, community trust, regulatory legitimacy, and corruption controls. You do not need to be a manufacturer or a utility to be exposed. A public agency can face continuity issues when heat affects staffing and service delivery, when wildfire smoke impacts outdoor operations, or when extreme weather damages assets. A school district can see impacts on attendance and learning tied to heat and air quality, and a spike in facility costs tied to HVAC and resilience upgrades. A hospital can face supply disruptions, utility instability, and staffing impacts during climate-driven events. A city can face infrastructure strain, insurance pricing shocks, and capital planning gaps.

The IPCC's synthesis report makes clear that climate change is already driving widespread impacts and increasing risks, and that these risks escalate with additional warming (IPCC, 2023). That matters for risk leaders because physical risk is not just a future scenario. It is an exposure pattern. And transition risk is not just about policy. It includes shifts in technology, market expectations, financing conditions, and legal standards that can change the value or viability of assets and business models (IFRS Foundation, 2023b).

If you strip away the terminology, sustainability risk becomes familiar. It is asset risk, workforce risk, third-party risk, business interruption risk, regulatory risk, and liability risk, operating on longer horizons and interacting across systems. It belongs in ERM because it affects strategy and performance, not because it makes a company look good (COSO, 2017).

ESG is messy, but the underlying demand is not going away

A lot of executives have whiplash. One year, ESG is a "must-have." The next year, it is treated like a political liability. Risk leaders have to operate in the real world, not the headlines. The reality is that the demand for comparable, decision-useful sustainability information is still pushing forward in global standards and investor expectations, even while specific laws get contested and adjusted.

The IFRS Foundation's ISSB standards are one signal of that direction. IFRS S1 (general sustainability-related disclosure requirements) and IFRS S2 (climate-related disclosures) are effective for reporting periods beginning on or after January 1, 2024, with adoption depending on jurisdiction (IFRS Foundation, 2023a; IFRS Foundation, 2023b). The TCFD has completed its remit and disbanded, with the ISSB standards positioned as the culmination of that work (IFRS Foundation, 2023c). This is not about agreeing with every ESG debate. It is about the fact that global capital markets increasingly want structured disclosure around governance, strategy, risk management, and metrics and targets.

At the same time, Europe's approach has emphasized broader corporate sustainability reporting obligations through CSRD and ESRS, including concepts such as double materiality. But the EU has also been actively revisiting the scope and burden of these requirements, with late 2025 votes and negotiations pointing toward scale-backs and delays for some firms (European Commission, n.d.; Reuters, 2025a; Reuters, 2025b). That creates two practical challenges. First, organizations that operate globally face mismatched expectations. Second, even when formal requirements soften, customers and investors often continue to require transparency through supply chains and procurement standards.

In the U.S., the SEC's March 2025 decision to end the defense of its climate disclosure rules underscores how quickly the federal posture can change (SEC, 2025). In California, climate disclosure rules have been contested in court, and parts of the regulatory package have been temporarily blocked, while other parts remain on track or move forward on different timelines (The Wall Street Journal, 2025). The message for risk leaders is not "wait until it settles." The message is "build a defensible capability that can survive the swings."

The risk leader's job: translate sustainability into enterprise risk language

Sustainability becomes actionable when it is translated into the same governance language used for financial, operational, and strategic risk. ISO 31000 emphasizes risk as the effect of uncertainty on objectives and stresses integration, tailoring, and continual improvement (ISO, 2018). COSO ERM emphasizes integrating risk with strategy and performance and building a culture and reporting structure that supports decisions (COSO, 2017). Sustainability risk fits both.

A practical translation looks like this:

Physical risk becomes business interruption and asset degradation risk. Transition risk becomes regulatory, market, and financing risk. Nature risk becomes supply chain vulnerability and operational dependency risk, especially in sectors dependent on land, water, and raw materials (TNFD, 2023). Social risk becomes workforce stability, community trust, and legal exposure risk. Governance risk becomes control failures, misstatement risk, fraud risk, and reputational collapse risk.

Once translated, the next step is to assign ownership and build controls. The biggest failure pattern I see is sustainability risk treated as a "program" owned by a sustainability office without a strong line into risk governance, internal controls, procurement, finance, legal, and operations. That structure creates two problems. It isolates data from decision-making, and it turns reporting into a scramble rather than a discipline.

Risk leaders do not have to become climate scientists. They have to become integrators. They connect the technical experts, the operational owners, the finance team, and the disclosure obligations into a system that produces consistent decisions and defensible documentation.

Materiality: financial materiality, double materiality, and the practical middle

Materiality becomes contentious quickly, but the practical point is straightforward. Organizations need a repeatable way to decide what sustainability topics are significant enough to be managed, measured, and disclosed. Under ISSB standards, the orientation is toward sustainability-related risks and opportunities that could reasonably be expected to affect the entity's prospects and enterprise value, which aligns with investor-focused financial materiality (IFRS Foundation, 2023a). Under GRI, the emphasis is on impacts on the economy, environment, and people, which aligns with impact materiality and stakeholder expectations (GRI, 2021). CSRD and ESRS incorporate double materiality concepts, even as implementation details evolve (European Commission, n.d.).

Instead of turning this into a philosophy debate, risk leaders should ask two disciplined questions. First, what sustainability factors can materially affect our objectives, costs, continuity, and legal exposure over relevant time horizons? Second, what impacts do we have that are significant enough to create regulatory, customer, workforce, or reputational consequences if unmanaged or misrepresented?

Those two questions capture the practical middle. They also reduce the risk of "checkbox materiality," where organizations choose easy topics and ignore hard ones. The worst version of ESG is when companies report what is convenient and stay silent on what is material.

Data, controls, and assurance: ESG is becoming an internal controls problem

A decade ago, many ESG reports were narrative-heavy. Today, the direction of travel is toward structured metrics, management processes, and comparability. That means ESG is turning into a data governance issue and, in many organizations, an internal controls issue. If your disclosures are used by investors, customers, lenders, or regulators, then the quality of your data and the integrity of your process matter.

This is where risk management can add real value. The same thinking used for financial reporting controls can be adapted for sustainability reporting controls. You define data owners. You document methodologies. You manage change. You validate inputs. You monitor exceptions. You set sign-off points. You retain evidence. You create audit trails.

If you have ever been in a claims deposition or a public records fight, you already know why this matters. People will ask, "How did you calculate that?" "Who approved it?" "What did you know and when?" A sustainability claim can become a liability claim when it is overstated, inconsistent, or unsupported. Greenwashing risk is not just reputational. It can be legal, contractual, and financial.

The push toward stronger standards makes this more urgent. ISSB standards are explicit about governance, strategy, risk management, and metrics and targets, and they are designed to support decision-useful disclosure (IFRS Foundation, 2023a; IFRS Foundation, 2023b). Separately, the ISSB has also been moving to enhance SASB standards, which reinforces the direction toward industry-specific, decision-useful metrics (IFRS Foundation, 2025).

So even if an organization decides to keep sustainability reporting voluntary, the defensible approach is to treat key metrics as if they might be challenged. Because at some point, they probably will be.

Supply chain and third-party risk: sustainability shows up where you outsource

Many organizations have less control over their risk profile than they think. They outsource operations, buy services, rely on vendors, and extend their footprint through contracts. That is where sustainability risks show up in practical ways: forced labor allegations in supply chains, vendors failing during extreme weather, third parties failing to meet emissions or reporting requirements, or suppliers losing insurance and passing costs downstream.

This is why procurement is becoming a frontline risk function. The supply chain will increasingly be asked for emissions data, human rights policies, and proof of controls. Even when formal regulation is delayed or narrowed, customer requirements can make it functionally mandatory. That is especially true for vendors that sell into larger enterprises or operate across borders.

A good sustainability risk approach treats third-party sustainability data the same way it treats cybersecurity attestations. You do not accept glossy claims without verification. You define minimum requirements. You prioritize critical vendors. You ask for evidence. You revisit it annually. You document exceptions. You escalate when necessary.

This is also where nature-related risk enters the picture. TNFD's framework is aimed at helping organizations assess and disclose dependencies and impacts on nature, structured around governance, strategy, risk and impact management, and metrics and targets (TNFD, 2023). Even if your organization is not ready to adopt TNFD, the concept is useful: many supply chains depend on ecosystem services, water, and land stability. Nature risk is not "extra." It is another lens on operational dependency.

Scenario thinking and resilience: stop pretending the future will be linear

One reason sustainability belongs in risk management is that it forces longer-horizon thinking. That does not mean forecasting exact outcomes. It means building readiness for a range of plausible conditions. Scenario analysis is often discussed in climate reporting contexts, and it can be overdone. But the core idea is solid: test your strategy and operations against conditions that would stress them.

For example, what happens to your service delivery if the number of extreme heat days doubles over the next decade? What happens to workforce availability, overtime, equipment reliability, and public-facing incidents? What happens to capital planning if insurance costs spike or coverage tightens for certain assets? What happens if a key supplier cannot deliver because of a regional disaster? What happens if a major customer requires verified emissions data as a condition of contract renewal?

These are not abstract questions. They are continuity questions. And resilience is not just about emergency response. It is about the everyday capacity to operate under stress without breaking controls.

The IPCC's synthesis report emphasizes that risks increase with warming and that adaptation and mitigation actions can reduce risk, though limits exist and timing matters (IPCC, 2023). For risk managers, that translates into two responsibilities: reduce exposures where you can, and build adaptive capacity where you cannot.

The politics are noisy, but the risk is still real

One trap is assuming that if a regulation is delayed, the risk goes away. It does not. What changes is who enforces expectations. In some periods, regulators lead. In others, capital markets lead. In others, customers, insurers, and plaintiffs' attorneys lead.

In late 2025, Europe's sustainability agenda faced visible political pushback, with votes and negotiations aimed at narrowing the scope and easing burdens, and critics warning of reduced transparency (Reuters, 2025a; Reuters, 2025b). In the U.S., the SEC's decision to end defense of climate rules signals how quickly institutional priorities can shift (SEC, 2025). In California, legal challenges and injunctions have created uncertainty around the implementation of climate reporting obligations (The Wall Street Journal, 2025). This is the operating environment: mixed signals, contested requirements, and continued pressure for disclosure.

Risk leaders should treat this like any other volatility. You build capabilities that are useful across outcomes. Better data governance is proper regardless of politics. Stronger continuity planning is useful regardless of politics. Vendor resiliency standards are useful regardless of politics. Transparent board governance is useful regardless of politics. The point is not to chase the latest requirement. The point is to build a program that can adjust.

What strong sustainability risk governance looks like in practice

Good governance starts with clarity about roles. Sustainability risk should have executive sponsorship, but it also needs operational ownership. If emissions are material, someone in operations owns the levers. If workforce risks are material, HR and operations own the levers. If supply chain risk is material, procurement owns the levers. Risk management's job is to coordinate, challenge assumptions, align reporting with reality, and make sure the risk picture is integrated into strategy.

Strong governance also uses familiar risk tools. You define risk appetite, not in vague language, but in what tradeoffs you will and will not accept. You define thresholds for escalation. You define who approves exceptions. You define how risk is reported to leadership. You choose leading indicators that show whether controls are improving or degrading.

And you keep it grounded. Not every organization needs the same level of reporting complexity. But every organization needs a coherent way to answer basic questions: What are our material sustainability-related risks? What are we doing about them? How do we know it's working? Can we prove it?

Closing

Long-term thinking is now a risk requirement because the costs of short-term thinking are landing faster, and they are landing in more places than many leaders expected. Sustainability is not a "nice-to-have" initiative when physical risk threatens continuity, when transition dynamics reshape markets and financing, when procurement demands verified data, and when disclosure claims can create liability. The ESG label may continue to evolve, and regulatory requirements may continue to swing. Nevertheless, the core discipline does not change: identify material exposures, integrate them into ERM, build defensible controls and data, and make decisions that hold up when conditions shift.

If your organization wants a simple test, use this one. Look at your next five major decisions, capital projects, vendor contracts, policy changes, or strategic initiatives. Ask whether sustainability-related risks and dependencies were considered in a structured way, or whether they were treated as a side conversation. If it's a side conversation, you have a governance gap. And governance gaps are where losses hide.

References

COSO. (2017). *Enterprise risk management: Integrating with strategy and performance.* Committee of Sponsoring Organizations of the Treadway Commission.

European Commission. (n.d.). *Corporate sustainability reporting.*

GRI. (2021). *GRI 1: Foundation 2021.* Global Reporting Initiative.

IFRS Foundation. (2023a). *IFRS S1 General Requirements for Disclosure of Sustainability-related Financial Information.*

IFRS Foundation. (2023b). *IFRS S2 Climate-related Disclosures.*

IFRS Foundation. (2023c). *ISSB and TCFD.*

IFRS Foundation. (2025). *ISSB proposes comprehensive review of priority SASB Standards.*

IPCC. (2023). *Climate change 2023: Synthesis report.* Intergovernmental Panel on Climate Change.

ISO. (2018). *ISO 31000:2018 Risk management — Guidelines.* International Organization for Standardization.

Reuters. (2025a, December 10). *EU sustainability cutbacks make low-carbon leaders harder to spot.*

Reuters. (2025b, December 16). *EU Parliament approves deal to weaken corporate sustainability laws.*

SEC. (2025, March 27). *SEC votes to end defense of climate disclosure rules (Press Release 2025-58).* U.S. Securities and Exchange Commission.

Taskforce on Nature-related Financial Disclosures (TNFD). (2023). *TNFD recommendations (v1.0).*

The Wall Street Journal. (2025, November 20). *U.S. appeals court halts California rule mandating climate risk reporting.*

Chapter 16
Global Risk Management in an Interconnected World

Thinking locally in a world that never is

Global Risk Management in an Interconnected World

A few years ago, "global risk" sounded like something reserved for multinationals with offices in five countries and a legal team that never sleeps. Now it shows up in ordinary places. A school district waiting on delayed laptops. A city stuck in a procurement loop because a component is suddenly backordered worldwide. A hospital watching medication costs jump after a shipping disruption. A public agency dealing with a cyber incident that started with a vendor across the country, or across the ocean. The point is not that everyone needs a geopolitical unit. The point is that you are already living inside global systems, whether you signed up for it or not.

The uncomfortable truth is that a lot of organizations still treat global risk like weather. Something you talk about after it hits, not something you plan for. That mindset is expensive. It drives last minute purchasing, operational workarounds, staff burnout, and public frustration. It also creates a credibility problem. People can tolerate bad news. They struggle with the feeling that leadership never saw it coming, even when the signs were visible.

What I want you to hold onto is simple: global risk management is not about predicting headlines. It is about spotting dependencies, reducing avoidable fragility, and building options before you need them. The tools are not mysterious. Most are just disciplined habits, applied consistently: scanning, stress testing, supplier visibility, scenario thinking, and clear communication when uncertainty is real.

When "somewhere else" lands on your desk

Global risk becomes "local" through a handful of predictable channels.

Supply chains are the most obvious. Goods and parts come from somewhere, and "somewhere" is often farther away than we like to admit. The second channel is rules. Regulations, trade restrictions, privacy requirements, sanctions, and reporting standards change across borders and often collide in messy ways. The third channel is technology. A single platform, cloud provider, or vendor network can connect thousands of organizations, which means one vulnerability can travel fast. The fourth is people. Migration, workforce disruption, misinformation, and community trauma do not respect jurisdictional boundaries. The fifth is hazards. Climate and disaster risk are increasingly systemic, meaning the impact shows up in finance, infrastructure, insurance availability, and continuity planning, not only in emergency response (UNDRR, 2025).

If you lead risk in a city, district, healthcare system, university, or mid-sized employer, you do not need to "go global." You need to stop being surprised by global threads that are already in your work.

Geopolitical risk: instability as the baseline, not the exception

A helpful way to think about today's geopolitical environment is that coordination is weaker, rivalries are sharper, and economic tools are used as pressure tactics more often than in the recent past. Ian Bremmer and Nouriel Roubini described a "G-Zero" world as one where no single country or bloc consistently provides the kind of stabilizing leadership that makes global systems feel predictable (Bremmer & Roubini, 2011).

You do not need to be an expert in foreign policy to translate that into practical risk questions. You just need to accept that shocks are more frequent and the ripple effects are faster.

Here is what geopolitical risk looks like at ground level.

A tariff or export restriction changes pricing after your budget is approved. A sanctions regime complicates sourcing because a supplier's sub-supplier is suddenly on a restricted list. A conflict drives energy volatility, which raises project costs and squeezes operating budgets. A politically motivated cyber campaign targets a sector, and your organization becomes collateral damage through a shared vendor. Even if you never buy directly from overseas, you may rely on overseas manufacturing through domestic distributors. That is why the phrase "we source locally" often fails under pressure. The product may be local. The dependency usually is not.

The best organizations do not try to outguess geopolitics. They build a small set of standing questions into planning and procurement. Where does this critical item truly originate? How concentrated is the supplier market? What is the lead time under stress, not under normal conditions? If the supply is interrupted for 60 days, what breaks first? Those questions are not dramatic, but they change behavior.

Supply chains: efficiency is not resilience

The past decade made one lesson painfully clear. Supply chains optimized only for low cost and just-in-time delivery carry hidden risk. The World Bank's Logistics Performance Index work puts structure around why disruptions matter: trade logistics is a system of services and infrastructure, and when parts of that system seize up, the operational impacts cascade (World Bank, 2023).

OECD's work on supply chain resilience emphasizes the same broader point: resilience is not one tactic; it is a set of choices that balance agility, adaptability, and alignment across partners (OECD, 2025).

In practice, resilience usually comes down to five moves.

First, visibility. If you do not know your critical suppliers and their key dependencies, you are planning in the dark.

Second, concentration control. If you have one supplier for a critical input, that may be fine, but it needs to be treated as a deliberate risk decision, not an accident.

Third, time realism. Lead times in a spreadsheet are not the same as lead times in a disruption. Build schedules around stress conditions, not best-case conditions.

Fourth, substitution. If you cannot get the preferred product, what is the acceptable alternative, and who has the authority to approve it quickly?

Fifth, an inventory policy that is honest. "We cannot afford stock" sounds responsible until the first disruption forces emergency purchases at a premium, incurring overtime and downtime costs.

None of this means hoarding inventory or rejecting global trade. It means you stop pretending that the cheapest option is automatically the lowest risk option.

Regulatory fragmentation and compliance whiplash

Global risk is not only about disruptions. It is also about requirements that multiply across jurisdictions. Even organizations that operate in a single country can be drawn into global compliance through data flows, vendors, investors, donors, grants, or partnerships.

This is where many teams get stuck. They treat compliance as a checklist, but the real risks are inconsistency and timing. Rules can change faster than organizations can update policies and training. That creates whiplash, and whiplash creates two outcomes: shortcuts or paralysis.

A more useful framing is to treat regulatory change as a monitoring and governance problem. You are tracking what could change, how quickly it could affect your operations, and who owns the response. That aligns well with mainstream risk frameworks that emphasize integration with governance and decision making (COSO, 2017; ISO, 2018).

For cross-border work, also remember that "regulatory" can include expectations around responsible business conduct, labor standards, and supply chain due diligence. The OECD Guidelines for Multinational Enterprises are widely referenced as a baseline for risk-based due diligence expectations, even beyond classic compliance (OECD, 2023).

The practical lesson is not to fear regulation. It is to stop being late for it. Late compliance becomes reputational risk and operational risk at the same time.

Cyber risk: borders do not matter to attackers

Cyber is one of the clearest examples of "global risk made local." Your systems are connected to vendor systems, and vendor systems are connected to other systems. That means your risk posture includes your ecosystem, not just your internal controls.

NIST's Cybersecurity Framework 2.0 is helpful here because it keeps the focus on outcomes and governance rather than chasing tools. It also explicitly elevates "govern" as a core function, which matters because cybersecurity is not just an IT issue; it is a leadership and accountability issue (NIST, 2024).

If you are leading risk management, the question is not whether you have firewalls. The question is whether you can answer, in plain language, three things.

1. How do we decide what cyber risks we accept versus reduce?
2. How do we know whether critical vendors can recover quickly?
3. How will we operate if key systems are down for a week?

Those answers should exist before the incident. After the incident, it is too late.

Public health, continuity, and the reality of global rules

The pandemic taught organizations that public health risk is operational risk. It impacts staffing, demand patterns, supply availability, public expectations, and governance. It also highlighted how global health rules shape national response.

The International Health Regulations have been amended, including changes adopted in 2024 and entering into force later, with a focus on stronger collaboration and new alert concepts, such as a "pandemic emergency" (WHO, 2025).

You do not need to become a health agency to learn from that. You need to treat health disruption as a recurring scenario, not a once-in-a-lifetime event. That means continuity planning that assumes workforce instability, supplier interruptions, and communication challenges simultaneously.

Culture: the hidden multiplier in global risk

Culture is often dismissed as "soft." In global risk work, it is not soft at all. It determines how people interpret urgency, escalate issues, challenge decisions, and handle uncertainty.

Hofstede's work is frequently cited because it gives leaders a language for thinking about how hierarchy, uncertainty avoidance, and collectivism versus individualism influence workplace behavior across contexts (Hofstede, 2011). Erin Meyer's culture mapping work is popular for a reason, too: it helps teams anticipate friction in communication, feedback, and decision-making when norms differ (Meyer, 2014).

This matters because many "risk failures" are not technical. They are interpersonal. A vendor does not disclose a delay early because admitting problems is culturally penalized. A project team interprets silence as agreement, while the other side interprets silence as respectful disagreement. A leader expects direct escalation, but a partner expects concerns to be raised indirectly.

If you do global work, or even multicultural work inside one country, cultural competence is not a nice-to-have. It is part of your control environment.

A case illustration: the hidden global threads in a local project

Picture a regional healthcare organization upgrading its emergency communications and patient intake systems. The project looks local. The vendor is domestic. The budget is approved. The timeline seems reasonable.

Midway through implementation, three problems land at once.

A key hardware component is delayed because a sub-supplier relies on overseas manufacturing capacity that is constrained. A new data handling requirement applies because a cloud-based service routes certain data through a jurisdiction with stricter privacy rules. A cyber vulnerability bulletin flags a common software library used by the vendor's platform and patching it requires downtime during a high-demand period.

None of these problems is "owned" by the project manager. They spill across procurement, IT, compliance, operations, communications, and leadership. If the organization never talked about global dependencies up front, the response becomes reactive: rushed purchasing, contract amendments, schedule slips, leadership frustration, and public messaging that sounds defensive.

If global risk was part of early planning, the organization could have built options into the design: alternate components pre-approved, contract language requiring sub-supplier transparency, a staged implementation plan, and a clear governance path for urgent decisions.

That is what global risk management is at the local level. It is not about predicting each disruption. It is about reducing the number of ways you can be cornered.

Practical steps that fit real organizations

Much global risk advice is written for large companies. Most public agencies and mid-sized organizations need something more straightforward and repeatable.

Start by building a short "dependency map" for your most critical services. Not a glossy report. A working document that answers: what do we rely on that we do not control? Then assign ownership for monitoring the top dependencies, even if it is informal.

Second, update your risk register to include a small number of global scenarios that match your reality: supply chain disruption, trade restriction cost spikes, cross-border regulatory change, major cyber incident through a vendor, and climate-driven service disruption. Pair each scenario with an operational impact statement, not just a risk score.

Third, build contract expectations that support resilience. Ask vendors to describe continuity capabilities, incident notification timelines, and sub-supplier transparency for critical components. If they cannot answer, that is information.

Fourth, integrate global risk scanning into an existing rhythm. It can be as simple as a quarterly discussion that uses a short set of prompts: what has changed in our supplier landscape, regulatory environment, cyber environment, and hazard exposure?

Fifth, practice communication. The Global Risks Report continues to emphasize how interconnected risks can compound and how social trust and information quality affect resilience (World Economic Forum, 2025). In plain terms, people want honest updates, with clear next steps, and no false certainty.

Closing: local stewardship in a global storm

The biggest trap in global risk work is thinking it requires a global-sized organization to do it well. It does not. What it requires is disciplined curiosity about dependencies, and the humility to plan for disruption without turning every plan into a disaster movie.

If you can name your critical external dependencies, monitor a few meaningful signals, and build options into procurement, technology, and continuity, you are already doing global risk management. You are doing it in a way that fits your scale. That is the goal. Not perfection, not prediction, just fewer surprises that turn into emergencies.

References

Bremmer, I., & Roubini, N. (2011). *A G-Zero World: The New Economic Club Will Produce Conflict, Not Cooperation. Foreign Affairs.*

Committee of Sponsoring Organizations of the Treadway Commission. (2017). *Enterprise Risk Management: Integrating with Strategy and Performance.*

Hofstede, G. (2011). Dimensionalizing cultures: The Hofstede model in context. *Online Readings in Psychology and Culture.*

International Monetary Fund. (2025). *World Economic Outlook, October 2025.*

International Organization for Standardization. (2018). *ISO 31000:2018 Risk management — Guidelines.*

Meyer, E. (2014). *The Culture Map: Breaking Through the Invisible Boundaries of Global Business.* PublicAffairs.

National Institute of Standards and Technology. (2024). *The NIST Cybersecurity Framework (CSF) 2.0 (CSWP 29).*

Organisation for Economic Co-operation and Development. (2023). *OECD Guidelines for Multinational Enterprises on Responsible Business Conduct.*

Organisation for Economic Co-operation and Development. (2025). *OECD Supply Chain Resilience Review: Navigating Risks.*

United Nations Office for Disaster Risk Reduction. (2025). *Global Assessment Report on Disaster Risk Reduction 2025.*

World Bank. (2023). *Connecting to Compete 2023: Trade Logistics in an Uncertain Global Economy.*

World Economic Forum. (2025). *The Global Risks Report 2025 (20th ed.).*

World Health Organization. (2025). *Amended International Health Regulations enter into force.*

Part: VI - Implementation, Measurement, and the Road Ahead

Chapter 17
Law, Policy, and the Risk Management Landscape

What leaders really need to know (without going to law school)

What leaders really need to know (without going to law school)

Most leaders do not get tripped up because they "ignored the law." They get tripped up because the law was only one part of the situation, and they treated it like the whole situation.

Here is what it usually looks like in real life. A supervisor tries to solve a behavior problem quickly and ends up walking straight into a disability accommodation issue (U.S. Equal Employment Opportunity Commission [EEOC], 2002). A department tries to "handle it internally" after a threat or violent incident and misses a training or documentation requirement that later becomes the center of a claim (Cal. Lab. Code § 6401.9, 2024). A city fixes the highest-profile potholes but cannot explain its prioritization process, so what should have been a hard conversation becomes a negligence conversation (League of California Cities, 2003). Or an agency does the right thing operationally, then loses credibility because emails and meeting records make it look careless or inconsistent (Cal. Gov't Code § 7920.000, 2024; BBK Law, 2025).

Law and policy are not just "compliance." They shape how your organization is judged after the fact. They influence what you must do, what you are allowed to do, what you can defend, and what a judge, regulator, board, union, or community member will expect you to have done. They also influence how risk managers should speak. The job is not to sound like a lawyer. The job is to make decisions that hold up when the room gets tense, and the story gets retold by people who were not there.

This chapter is educational, not legal advice. The point is to help leaders know what questions to ask and what habits to build so you can partner with counsel effectively and keep surprises to a minimum.

Keys

Law sets the floor for what you must do, but your policies, training promises, contracts, and past practices often set the standard you will actually be held to. Workers' compensation changes how injury cases move, but it does not erase operational accountability. For public entities, transparency rules mean documentation is not optional, and sloppy documentation can become the story. Privacy laws and cybersecurity expectations now sit inside everyday risk work, not off to the side. Most importantly, the leaders who stay out of trouble are not perfect; they are consistent, they can explain their decisions, and their written record matches what they really do.

Law is the floor, your program is the ceiling

A helpful way to think about law is that it defines minimum duties and minimum rights. It tells you what cannot be ignored. In workplace health and safety, for example, the federal OSH Act's General Duty Clause expects employers to provide a workplace "free from recognized hazards" likely to cause death or serious physical harm (Occupational Safety and Health Administration, n.d.; U.S. Department of Labor, n.d.). That is a baseline expectation, not a whole playbook.

Many organizations make two mistakes here.

The first is treating the law like a checklist. They focus on proving they "covered" something rather than building a system that actually reduces harm. That approach tends to collapse under stress because real incidents do not arrive as neat categories. They arrive as messy human situations with competing demands.

The second mistake is assuming that the law is the only standard. In practice, what you said you would do often matters as much as what the law requires. If your policy says supervisors will conduct weekly inspections, document hazards, and track corrective action, then you created a promise. If you do not follow it, plaintiffs, regulators, unions, and auditors do not need to prove you violated a regulation to argue you were careless. They can argue you violated your own standard of care, and your documents will back them up (Goldberg, 2001).

This is why high-performing risk programs pay attention to the law, then build beyond it. They treat compliance as the start line, not the finish line.

The difference between law, policy, procedure, and practice

This sounds basic, but it is one of the most expensive misunderstandings in organizations.

Law is external. It comes from statutes, regulations, case law, and sometimes local ordinances or agency rules. It is enforced by regulators, courts, or oversight bodies. It can change, and it can be interpreted differently depending on the facts.

Policy is your organization's statement of intent and boundaries. It answers: What do we believe? What do we require? Who is accountable? What decisions are we making consistently across the organization?

Procedure is the "how." It translates policy into steps, roles, tools, forms, timelines, and documentation.

Practice is what actually happens on Tuesday at 3:40 p.m. when the field is short-staffed and someone is upset.

Your risk exposure often lives in the gaps between those layers. If the law requires training, your policy promises training, your procedure describes training, but your practice is "we will get to it later," the system is lying. And the first time you need to defend it, that gap becomes obvious.

California's workplace violence prevention requirements are a clear example. The statute requires a Workplace Violence Prevention Plan and training that includes an opportunity for interactive questions and answers with a knowledgeable person (Cal. Lab. Code § 6401.9, 2024). Many organizations can produce a plan. Fewer can show that training was delivered in a way that actually matched the plan, addressed site hazards, and allowed real interaction. That mismatch is where trouble starts, not the existence of a document.

Cal/OSHA's model plan is not "the law," but it reflects the shape and substance regulators expect to see when they evaluate a program (California Department of Industrial Relations, Division of Occupational Safety and Health, n.d.). If your plan looks good on paper but your incident log, training approach, or corrective actions do not line up, the credibility gap becomes the problem.

The litigation lens: duty, reasonableness, and the record you leave behind

When something goes wrong, your organization will be judged through a particular lens. In negligence, the classic elements are duty, breach, causation, and damages, with "duty of reasonable care" sitting near the center of how courts think about responsibility (Goldberg, 2001). You do not need to be a tort scholar to lead well, but you do need to understand the practical implication: people will ask what a reasonable organization would have done under similar circumstances.

That is why documentation matters. Not the performative kind, not the "cover yourself" kind, but the kind that shows what you knew, what you decided, why you decided it, and what you did next.

In court, records are not just paperwork. They can become evidence. Rules like the federal business records exception exist because records created in the regular course of activity are often treated as reliable (Fed. R. Evid. 803(6); Cornell Law School Legal Information

Institute, n.d.). California has a similar concept in its Evidence Code (Cal. Evid. Code § 1271, 2024). The details are for attorneys, but the management implication is simple: the notes you keep can travel farther than you think.

This is where leaders sometimes freeze. They worry that documenting mistakes will be used against them, so they stop documenting. That usually makes things worse. A thin file does not look like "we were careful." It often looks like "we did not have control."

A better approach is to train people to document like professionals:

- Write in plain, factual language.
- Describe observable behavior and conditions, not motives.
- Separate facts from conclusions.
- Capture the corrective action and timeline.
- Avoid sarcasm or moral commentary, especially in email.

This is not about fear. It is about discipline. Documentation is a leadership habit, not a compliance chore.

Workers' compensation and the tradeoff leaders misunderstand

Workers' compensation is often described as a bargain. Employees receive no-fault access to medical care and wage replacement for work-related injuries and illnesses. In exchange, employers generally receive protection from tort lawsuits for those injuries, under the exclusive remedy doctrine (Baker, 1986; Vieweg, 1981).

Leaders sometimes hear "exclusive remedy" and assume the risk is contained. It is contained in one sense, but not erased.

First, the costs still land somewhere. They show up in medical payments, indemnity, reserves, excess layers, and experience rating impacts, or for public entities and pools, in long-tail liabilities that quietly crowd out future services. The injury may not become a jury verdict, but it can become a budget story.

Second, workers' compensation does not protect you from everything. Different jurisdictions recognize different exceptions and pathways. Some extreme fact patterns can still spill into civil litigation, and some claims involve third parties, premises, or product issues that are not neatly contained by comp. The details depend on jurisdiction, but the leadership point is consistent: comp changes the legal lane, it does not remove the obligation to prevent harm (Baker, 1986; Vieweg, 1981).

Third, comp cases are rarely just "comp cases." They overlap with leave laws, disability accommodations, performance management, and sometimes discipline. The moment you start mixing those issues, you need coordination.

For example, the ADA requires an interactive process and reasonable accommodation analysis, and the EEOC's guidance gives practical direction on what that process looks like (EEOC, 2002). The FMLA has its own rules and timelines (U.S. Department of Labor, 2023). California readers may also be navigating CFRA alongside FMLA, which increases the need for HR and legal alignment. If you treat these as separate silos, you create inconsistent decisions. Inconsistent decisions are what get challenged.

The risk leader's role is not to practice employment law. It is to make sure the system is coherent: the claim process, the return-to-work program, the accommodation process, and the supervisory documentation should not contradict each other.

Government liability is different, but it is not a free pass

Public entities operate inside a different legal architecture than private organizations. Immunities, claim presentation requirements, and procedural rules shape what claims can proceed and how (League of California Cities, 2003). Many jurisdictions require administrative claims before lawsuits and impose short timelines for certain claim types (Sacramento Superior Court, n.d.). If your organization misses a procedural step, it can change the path of a case entirely.

Leaders sometimes misread this and think immunity means safety can be treated as optional. That is a costly mistake. Immunity is not a moral shield. It is a legal framework that still expects reasoned governance.

Courts often distinguish between discretionary policy decisions and operational acts. High-level allocation decisions may be more protected, while day-to-day implementation failures are less protected, especially when they contradict established standards or when hazards are known and unmanaged (League of California Cities, 2003). The practical lesson is this: you want to be able to show that your organization makes decisions with a consistent method.

That means you can explain prioritization. You can show how hazards are identified, how work is scheduled, and how constraints are managed. You can show you took known risks seriously, even when resources were limited. This is where good risk management looks like good governance.

Transparency and public trust live in the same file cabinet

For public agencies, transparency laws change the way risk work must be documented and communicated.

At the federal level, FOIA creates broad access to federal agency records, subject to exemptions (Freedom of Information Act, 5 U.S.C. § 552, 2022; U.S. Department of Justice, 2022). In California, the California Public Records Act provides access to public records, and it was reorganized and renumbered into Government Code § 7920.000 and related sections (Cal. Gov't Code § 7920.000, 2024; First Amendment Coalition, 2023). That reorganization is not just a trivia point. It affects how policies and counsel refer to the law, how staff search for exemptions, and how agencies train people to respond properly.

Open meeting laws add another layer. The Brown Act reflects the core premise that local government deliberations and actions should be conducted openly, with defined exceptions (BBK Law, 2025; Bay Area Urban Areas Security Initiative, 2012). If your risk decisions are discussed in meetings, your process needs to respect those rules, and your written record needs to be able to withstand public scrutiny.

For risk managers and leaders, this means two things.

First, you cannot treat documentation as private by default. Assume that some portion of what you write may become public. That does not mean you should stop writing. It means you should write like a professional who expects accountability.

Second, transparency pressures can tempt leaders to manage optics instead of managing risk. That is backwards. The better move is to build real processes that generate defensible records. When your method is solid, the record becomes an asset rather than a threat.

Privacy is now a frontline risk issue, not an IT issue

If risk leaders used to think privacy was a specialist concern, that era is over. Organizations collect more data, share it more widely, store it longer, and rely on vendors more heavily than they realize. That includes employee data, customer data, student data, patient data, camera footage, access logs, vehicle telematics, and incident records.

California's consumer privacy framework gives consumers rights over the personal information that businesses collect, and the Attorney General's office provides guidance and regulations to support implementation (California Department of Justice, 2024). Statutory sections such as California Civil Code § 1798.100 describe notice and handling expectations around personal information and third-party sharing (Cal. Civ. Code § 1798.100, 2024). Even if your organization is not a classic "consumer business," many public and quasi-public organizations still touch systems and vendors that must comply.

If you operate internationally or use vendors that do, the GDPR's principles emphasize lawful and transparent processing and data minimization concepts that influence global expectations (Regulation (EU) 2016/679, 2016). You do not need to memorize the GDPR, but you should recognize what it represents: privacy has become a core governance topic.

From a risk management perspective, privacy is not just "avoid a fine." It is operational resilience. When you have a breach, a public records request, a lawsuit, or a labor dispute, the quality of your data governance shows up fast. What did you collect? Why? Where is it stored? Who has access? What does the vendor contract say? How quickly can you retrieve it? How quickly can you delete it if required?

This is also where legal, policy, and technology intersect in ways that can surprise leaders. A safety incident can trigger a records request. A records request can trigger a privacy review. A privacy review can expose weak retention practices. Weak retention practices can trigger litigation risk. That chain reaction happens all the time.

Contracts and procurement: the quiet place where risk gets created

Some of the biggest exposures are not created by your employees. They come from vendors, contractors, and partners.

Contracts are where you allocate responsibilities and financial risk. This includes indemnity language, insurance requirements, additional insured status, primary and non-contributory wording, and the responsibilities for safety, supervision, and compliance. If that language is vague, outdated, or inconsistent across departments, you end up paying for someone else's mistake or discovering that the insurance you thought would respond does not respond.

The leadership habit here is simple. High-risk contracts should be reviewed by the people who understand risk transfer, and departments should not be left to invent their own templates. If procurement is decentralized, you need a centralized checklist. If project managers treat contract language as boilerplate, you need to show them how it turns into claim outcomes.

This is also where policy matters. Your contract requirements are effectively a policy statement. If you require vendors to do certain training, maintain certain documentation, or follow certain safety standards, you should be prepared to verify that those things happened. Otherwise, you have created another paper-versus-practice gap.

When laws change, the real work is translating change into behavior

Regulatory change rarely fails because leaders did not hear about it. It fails because organizations do not translate it into supervisor behavior, training design, and field-level execution.

Workplace violence prevention is a good example because it forces organizations to take a real human risk seriously while also meeting defined structural requirements. California's law requires plans and training elements, and it specifically calls out interactive questions and answers with a knowledgeable person (Cal. Lab. Code § 6401.9, 2024). That is not a "checkbox." It is a design requirement. It changes how you deliver training and how you prove training happened.

Cal/OSHA's model plan provides a reference for what a meaningful plan contains, and it emphasizes the operational pieces: hazard identification, procedures for reporting, incident response, post-incident review, and recordkeeping (California Department of Industrial Relations, Division of Occupational Safety and Health, n.d.). The law is not asking for a document that sits on a shelf. It is asking for a system that is alive.

The leadership move is to treat regulatory change as an implementation project, not a memo. Who owns it? What changes in the field? What changes in supervisor coaching? What changes in documentation? What does "good" look like? How will you audit it without making it feel like punishment?

That same translation challenge shows up in many areas: heat illness prevention, ergonomics, infectious disease controls, ADA interactive process, leave coordination, driver safety, cyber incident reporting, and more. The organizations that handle change well build a habit of revisiting policy and training on a cycle, not only after something goes wrong.

How risk leaders partner with legal without turning everything into legal

A common failure mode is either avoiding legal until it is too late or sending everything to legal so leaders stop thinking. Both approaches are expensive.

The better approach is partnership with clean roles.

Legal counsel helps interpret obligations, privileges, liabilities, and strategy. Risk leaders help translate that guidance into systems that actually work in the field. Operations leaders help design what is doable. HR helps integrate the human side. Finance helps price the choices. When those voices are aligned early, organizations move faster and defend better.

A practical way to make this partnership work is to bring counsel-focused questions rather than open-ended panic. For example:

- What is the minimum required by law here, and what do we recommend as best practice beyond that minimum?
- Which parts of this documentation could be disclosable under public records rules, and how should we handle privileged communications?
- If we write this policy, are we creating obligations we cannot reliably meet?
- What exceptions or timelines apply if this becomes a claim against the entity?
- What are the top two ways this goes wrong in litigation, and what records would help us defend it?

Those questions keep leaders in leadership mode. They also keep the organization from building policies that sound great and fail in practice.

Closing: make your risk decisions explainable

Law, policy, and risk management are not separate subjects. They are three ways of asking the same question: what do we owe people, what do we promise, and can we prove we lived up to it?

If you want a simple standard for this chapter, it is this. Make your decisions explainable. Not just to your boss, but to a neutral outsider who shows up later with incomplete context and hard questions. Explainable decisions come from consistent processes, practical policies, real training, and documentation that matches reality.

Two reflection prompts to carry forward: Where are we relying on "tribal knowledge" when the law expects a system? And where have we written policies that describe the organization we wish we had, instead of the one we can reliably run today?

References

Baker, B. A. (1986). *Worker's compensation: Using the exclusive remedy doctrine as a shield from tort liability*. University of Wyoming College of Law, Land and Water Law Review.

Bay Area Urban Areas Security Initiative. (2012). *Open meeting laws in California: Ralph M. Brown Act*.

BBK Law. (2025). *The Brown Act: The people's business and the right to attend public meetings*.

California Civil Code § 1798.100 (2024).

California Department of Industrial Relations, Division of Occupational Safety and Health. (n.d.). *Cal/OSHA's model workplace violence prevention plan*.

California Department of Justice. (2024). *California Consumer Privacy Act (CCPA)*.

California Evidence Code § 1271 (2024).

California Government Code § 7920.000 (2024).

California Labor Code § 6401.9 (2024).

Cornell Law School Legal Information Institute. (n.d.). *Federal Rules of Evidence, Rule 803*.

Fed. R. Evid. 803(6).

First Amendment Coalition. (2023). *California Public Records Act primer*.

Freedom of Information Act, 5 U.S.C. § 552 (2022).

Goldberg, J. C. P. (2001). The Restatement (Third) and the place of duty in negligence law. *Vanderbilt Law Review, 54*(3).

League of California Cities. (2003). *The Tort Claims Act (Government Claims Act) materials*.

Occupational Safety and Health Administration. (n.d.). *OSH Act of 1970: Section 5, Duties (General Duty Clause)*.

Regulation (EU) 2016/679 of the European Parliament and of the Council (General Data Protection Regulation). (2016).

Sacramento Superior Court. (n.d.). *Government Claims Act*.

U.S. Department of Justice. (2022). *Freedom of Information Act, 5 U.S.C. § 552*.

U.S. Department of Labor. (2023). *Fact Sheet #28: The Family and Medical Leave Act.*

U.S. Department of Labor. (n.d.). *Employment Law Guide: Occupational Safety and Health.*

U.S. Equal Employment Opportunity Commission. (2002). *Enforcement guidance: Reasonable accommodation and undue hardship under the Americans with Disabilities Act.*

Vieweg, W. F. (1981). Erosion of the workers' compensation exclusive remedy doctrine. *Defense Counsel Journal.*

Chapter 18

Measuring What Matters – ROI and Continuous Improvement

Turning safety from a cost center into a strategic engine

Turning safety from a cost center into a strategic engine

If you want to know whether an organization is serious about safety, do not start with the posters, the slogans, or the annual training calendar. Start with what gets measured, what gets discussed in leadership meetings, and what gets funded when budgets get tight. Measurement is where intentions turn into priorities. It is also where safety either becomes a checkbox or becomes a disciplined way of running the operation.

Most leaders say they care about safety. The friction shows up when someone asks, "What did we get for the money?" That question is fair. Safety competes with staffing, equipment, projects, and service delivery. But it is also a trap when ROI is treated like a narrow spreadsheet exercise. Some benefits show up quickly in claims costs and downtime. Others show up slowly as fewer catastrophic events, better retention, better productivity, and fewer "surprises" that derail operations. The goal is not to force everything into a perfect formula. The goal is to measure enough, in the right way, that leadership can make decisions it can defend.

The core idea of this chapter is simple: safety becomes strategic when you treat it like a continuous improvement system, not a compliance program. That means linking safety to business outcomes, using a balanced set of leading and lagging indicators, and building a feedback loop that actually changes how work gets done (Deming, 1986; ISO, 2015; ISO, 2018). It also means being honest about what you can quantify, what you can estimate, and what you must still choose because it is the right obligation to workers and the public.

Key learnings in narrative form

Safety ROI works best when framed as cost control and operational reliability, not just claims reduction. Leading indicators matter because they show whether risk is building before the injury happens, while lagging indicators tell you what already went wrong (Hopkins, 2009; Heinrich, Petersen, & Roos, 1980). Continuous improvement only functions when corrective actions are tracked to closure and verified in the field; otherwise, the same problems recycle with different labels (Deming, 1986; Juran & Godfrey, 1999). Strong measurement systems also guard against false confidence by checking data quality, normalizing for exposure, and identifying unintended consequences, such as underreporting (Probst & Estrada, 2010; Zohar, 1980).

Why ROI language matters, and why it gets misused

ROI is a powerful tool because it speaks the language of executives, boards, and finance teams. But it gets misused in two common ways.

The first misuse is treating ROI as a demand for certainty. In the real world, you rarely have perfect data, and you cannot run controlled experiments on people's injuries. You make decisions under uncertainty. Risk management exists because of that uncertainty (ISO, 2018). If leadership insists on "prove it to the penny" before acting, prevention becomes permanently delayed, and the organization quietly accepts higher losses.

The second misuse is treating ROI as only financial. Injury costs include direct and indirect costs. Direct costs are the obvious ones like medical treatment and indemnity. Indirect costs include overtime, disruption, supervisor time, retraining, equipment damage, administrative burden, morale impacts, and service delays. Those indirect costs are real, even when they do not land in a single budget line (Fleming, 2001; Hinze, 1997). A strong risk leader helps finance and operations see both.

A more realistic approach is to use ROI as part of a broader value case. Some interventions will show a clean financial payback. Some are justified because they reduce catastrophic potential. Some are justified because they improve reliability and throughput. Some are justified because they protect the organization's license to operate in the community. The point is to match the justification to the decision, instead of forcing every decision into the same narrow template.

Measuring what matters: the balance of lagging and leading indicators

Lagging indicators are the ones everyone knows: recordable rates, lost-time cases, severity rates, claim counts, total incurred, litigation rates, and days away or restricted. They are useful, but they are rear-view mirror metrics. They tell you what already happened. They also have a problem. In smaller organizations or smaller departments, rates can swing wildly based on one incident, which can lead leaders to overreact or, worse, declare victory too early.

Leading indicators are different. They measure conditions and behaviors that influence outcomes. They include things like hazard correction timeliness, quality of job hazard analyses, completion and verification of preventive maintenance, participation in safety walks, training effectiveness checks, near-miss reporting trends, supervisor coaching activity, inspection findings, and closure of corrective actions. Properly used, leading indicators show whether the system is getting healthier or more brittle (Hopkins, 2009; Zohar, 1980).

The mistake is treating leading indicators as "activity counts." Counting how many inspections you did is not the same as measuring whether inspections found meaningful hazards and whether those hazards were corrected. Counting training attendance is not the same as measuring competency. If leading indicators are just busywork metrics, they become performative and people learn to game them.

A practical measurement set usually includes both, and it connects them. If a department's severity is rising, you look upstream. Are hazards being corrected slower? Is overtime rising? Are inspections getting thinner? Are supervisors documenting less? Are certain tasks producing repeated strains? That is how you turn data into operational learning.

Exposure matters too. Comparing departments without normalizing for hours worked, miles driven, patient days, student contact hours, or work orders completed can mislead leadership. A small department can look "worse" simply because one event carries more weight. A high-volume unit can look "better" simply because its exposure is not properly accounted for. This is why measurement has to be built with basic statistical humility.

Turning incidents into improvement, not paperwork

Most organizations have incident investigations. Fewer have incident learning.

Investigation becomes paperwork when the goal is to close a file. Learning happens when the goal is to change conditions. A strong system asks, "What about the work made this outcome likely?" That includes equipment, environment, staffing, procedure clarity, supervision, training, fatigue, and competing demands. It also includes organizational signals: what was rewarded, what was tolerated, and what people believed would happen if they slowed down.

Continuous improvement depends on a feedback loop. Deming's Plan-Do-Study-Act cycle is still relevant because it is not about perfection; it is about learning and adjustment (Deming, 1986). ISO 45001 uses the same basic logic through planning, operational control, performance evaluation, and improvement (ISO, 2018). The cycle breaks when corrective actions are assigned but not resourced, or when closure is administrative rather than verified.

A simple discipline makes a big difference: corrective actions should have an owner, a due date, a clear success definition, and a verification step. Verification means someone checks the field, not the file. If a hazard was "corrected," you confirm the condition changed, and the workaround stopped. If training is "completed," you confirm that people can do the task safely. This is the difference between motion and progress.

There is also a cultural side. If incidents are used to punish, reporting drops. When reporting drops, the organization loses early warning and then gets blindsided later. Research on safety climate has long shown that perceptions of management priority and fairness influence safety behaviors and outcomes (Zohar, 1980; Neal & Griffin, 2006). If your measurement system rewards low numbers without checking reporting health, you create underreporting and self-deception.

The ROI toolkit: how to build a defensible value case

When leaders ask for ROI, they usually want three things: credibility, clarity, and a decision recommendation. You can deliver that without pretending you have perfect data.

A good value case starts by defining the problem in operational terms. "We have too many strains" is vague. "We have a pattern of back strains during unloading and moving materials, with X days away and high overtime coverage, and it's concentrated in three locations" is a decision-ready statement.

Next, identify the intervention and the mechanism. Are you changing equipment? Redesigning workflow? Adding mechanical assists? Updating staffing patterns? Improving preventive maintenance? Strengthening supervision? You want to show how the intervention changes exposure.

Then estimate benefits in layers.

Start with direct financial impact where you can: claim costs avoided, reduced overtime, reduced temporary staffing, reduced equipment damage, and reduced legal spend. Where you cannot be precise, use ranges and be transparent about assumptions. This is common in risk analysis and is more honest than fake precision (ISO, 2018).

Add operational benefits: fewer disruptions, improved cycle time, reduced rework, and fewer service delays. Continuous improvement literature emphasizes that quality and safety are not separate from performance. When processes are stable and controlled, output becomes more reliable (Deming, 1986; Juran & Godfrey, 1999).

Add risk reduction benefits that matter even if they are harder to quantify: reduced probability of catastrophic loss, reduced regulatory exposure, improved insurability, improved reputation, improved employee retention. Retention and engagement might sound soft, but turnover is expensive, and safety culture affects whether people stay, especially in high-stress roles (Neal & Griffin, 2006; Christian, Bradley, Wallace, & Burke, 2009).

Finally, define the measurement plan. What will you track to show whether the intervention worked? What will you look at after 30, 90, and 180 days? What would cause you to adjust the approach? This step is often missing, and it is what makes the ROI case defensible rather than rhetorical.

If you want an ROI structure that finance teams recognize, Phillips' ROI methodology is commonly used in training and program evaluation contexts because it separates outcomes, isolates effects where possible, and makes assumptions explicit (Phillips & Phillips, 2016). You do not need to implement it rigidly, but the discipline is valuable.

Continuous improvement in the real world: examples that leaders recognize

It helps to ground this in situations leaders actually face.

A public works division with repeat vehicle incidents

A city fleet shows a rise in backing incidents and minor collisions. The initial reaction is "drivers need training." Training is delivered. Incidents do not change.

A better approach looks at the system. Routes are adjusted without input. New equipment has different sightlines. Yard congestion is worse. Spotting expectations are unclear. Supervisors are inconsistent in coaching. Near misses are not reported because people fear discipline. When the division measures the upstream factors, it finds that yard layout and dispatch patterns are driving risk. It makes physical changes, sets a spotting rule, and measures compliance through periodic observation. Incidents decline, but just as important, the organization can explain why.

This is the improvement lesson: do not measure only the outcome. Measure the conditions that produce the outcome.

A school district with rising custodial strains

A district sees an increase in strains in custodial work. The data shows the injuries cluster around floor care tasks and moving supplies. The district invests in better equipment, but the injuries continue because staff are still using old workarounds and rushing due to time pressure.

Continuous improvement looks at workflow and staffing. The district adjusts schedules, builds micro-breaks into high-load shifts, and standardizes how supplies are staged to reduce repeated heavy lifts. It also measures hazard correction speed and supervisor check-ins, not just claim counts. Over time, severity drops because exposure drops.

A hospital dealing with sharps' injuries and reporting fatigue

A hospital has sharps injuries and inconsistent reporting. Leadership tries messaging. Nothing changes.

Improvement begins by mapping the process: where do injuries happen, when do they happen, what equipment is used, and what barriers exist to reporting? The organization changes device selection, improves disposal placement, and simplifies reporting. It measures reporting timeliness and feedback loops so staff see that reports lead to changes. That improves both safety outcomes and trust.

All three examples share the same pattern: measurement drives learning, learning drives targeted action, and targeted action becomes visible to staff.

The governance side: keeping improvement alive after the spotlight moves on

Most safety programs do fine when leadership attention is high. The real test is what happens when attention shifts. Continuous improvement requires governance habits that protect the work.

ISO 45001 emphasizes performance evaluation, internal audit, and management review as structured ways to sustain improvement (ISO, 2018). Those concepts are useful even if you do not pursue certification. The leadership practice is to create a recurring rhythm where safety performance is reviewed like operational performance, not as a separate compliance report.

That rhythm should include a few consistent questions.

What are our top risk drivers right now, and how do we know?
Which corrective actions are overdue, and why?
Where are leading indicators trending the wrong way?
Where are we seeing weak signals, like reduced reporting or rising overtime?
What decisions are we making this month that increase or reduce risk?

When leaders ask these questions consistently, safety stops being a "departmental function" and becomes part of how the organization runs.

Closing

Turning safety from a cost center into a strategic engine is not about selling safety with fancy language. It is about building a measurement system that makes risk visible, makes improvement trackable, and makes leadership decisions defensible. ROI matters, but only when it is used with honesty and operational clarity. Continuous improvement matters, but only when corrective actions are real, verified, and sustained.

If you want two reflection prompts to carry forward, keep them simple. First, where are we measuring activity instead of measuring control health? Second, where do we keep paying for the same loss pattern because we never changed the conditions that produce it?

Safety becomes strategic when the answers to those questions lead to action, not just discussion.

References

Christian, M. S., Bradley, J. C., Wallace, J. C., & Burke, M. J. (2009). Workplace safety: A meta-analysis of the roles of person and situation factors. *Journal of Applied Psychology, 94*(5), 1103–1127.

Deming, W. E. (1986). *Out of the crisis*. MIT Press.

Fleming, M. (2001). *Accident prevention and risk control*. Health and Safety Executive.

Heinrich, H. W., Petersen, D., & Roos, N. (1980). *Industrial accident prevention: A safety management approach* (5th ed.). McGraw-Hill.

Hinze, J. (1997). *Construction safety*. Prentice Hall.

Hopkins, A. (2009). *Thinking about process safety indicators*. Safety Science, 47(4), 460–465.

International Organization for Standardization. (2015). *ISO 9001:2015 Quality management systems — Requirements*. ISO.

International Organization for Standardization. (2018). *ISO 31000:2018 Risk management — Guidelines*. ISO.

International Organization for Standardization. (2018). *ISO 45001:2018 Occupational health and safety management systems — Requirements with guidance for use*. ISO.

Juran, J. M., & Godfrey, A. B. (1999). *Juran's quality handbook* (5th ed.). McGraw-Hill.

Neal, A., & Griffin, M. A. (2006). A study of the lagged relationships among safety climate, safety motivation, safety behavior, and accidents at the individual and group levels. *Journal of Applied Psychology, 91*(4), 946–953.

Phillips, J. J., & Phillips, P. P. (2016). *Handbook of training evaluation and measurement methods* (4th ed.). Routledge.

Probst, T. M., & Estrada, A. X. (2010). Accident under-reporting among employees: Testing the moderating influence of psychological safety climate and supervisor enforcement of safety practices. *Accident Analysis & Prevention, 42*(5), 1438–1444.

Zohar, D. (1980). Safety climate in industrial organizations: Theoretical and applied implications. *Journal of Applied Psychology, 65*(1), 96–102.

Chapter 19
Implementing Your Risk Strategy

From Plans to Practice

Implementing Your Risk Strategy: From Plans to Practice

Most risk strategies read well. They have the right words, the right framework, and the right structure. The problem is that paper does not do the work. People do. And people are juggling deadlines, staffing gaps, politics, fatigue, competing priorities, and the quiet pressure to keep the wheels turning. That is where strategies go to die, not because they were wrong, but because they never became real in the places where work actually happens.

Implementation is not a single moment. It is a long series of small decisions made by supervisors, frontline staff, and managers who are trying to be reasonable under pressure. If your strategy cannot survive that environment, it is not a strategy yet. It is a plan.

This chapter is about closing the gap between intention and execution. Not with motivational posters or another binder, but with practical architecture: clear ownership, simple routines, visible feedback loops, and the discipline to keep doing the basics long after the kickoff meeting. Risk frameworks like ISO 31000 and COSO ERM stress integration into governance, decision-making, and performance. That word "integration" sounds abstract until you realize what it means in practice: risk has to show up in how you budget, hire, procure, train, maintain assets, manage vendors, investigate incidents, and make tradeoffs when time is tight (ISO, 2018; COSO, 2017).

The most important lessons here can be said in plain language. Implementation fails when accountability is vague, when leaders confuse activity with adoption, and when the organization does not build a cadence for follow-through. Implementation succeeds when you make the strategy easy to understand at the field level, when you remove friction from the right behaviors, and when you create feedback loops that help people see progress and learn from mistakes (Deming, 1986; Kotter, 1996; Hiatt, 2006). If you remember nothing else, remember this: the difference between a risk program that changes outcomes and one that does not is usually not intelligence. It is consistency.

The "strategy-to-practice" gap is predictable

Most organizations think their implementation problem is complexity. It is usually something else.

It is role confusion. People assume someone else owns the work.
It is overload. The strategy gets added on top of everything else without removing anything.

It is weak translation. The plan is written in enterprise language, but work happens in operational language.

It is invisible progress. Staff do not see what changed, so the strategy feels like talk.

It is inconsistent leadership. One leader pushes it, another leader shrugs, and people follow the shrug.

Behavioral science calls this bounded rationality. People do not optimize. They do what is workable with the time and attention they have (Simon, 1955). Implementation has to respect that. You cannot build a strategy that assumes infinite capacity and perfect compliance. You have to build one that survives human reality.

This is why execution is a design problem. You design who owns it, how it is monitored, how decisions are made, and how it becomes part of normal work. If those design choices are missing, people fill the gaps with improvisation. Improvisation is not always bad. But when the improvisation is the system, the system becomes fragile.

Start with governance that actually holds under pressure

A risk strategy becomes real when it is governed like something that matters. Governance does not mean more meetings. It means clear authority, clear decision rights, and clear accountability for follow-through.

COSO frames ERM as part of how organizations set strategy and manage performance, implying that risk leaders must be connected to the operational and financial conversations where trade-offs occur (COSO, 2017). ISO 31000 emphasizes leadership, integration, and continual improvement, which means risk cannot live as a separate lane. It has to be embedded (ISO, 2018). If your strategy lives only in the risk department, it will stay there.

In practical terms, governance should answer a few uncomfortable questions:

- Who has the authority to require corrective action, not just recommend it?
- Who owns risk decisions when operations and risk disagree?
- What happens when a department is overdue on a high-risk action?
- How do we decide which risks get funded this quarter?
- How do we keep priorities stable long enough for improvement to take hold?

If those questions are not answered, the organization will answer them informally. Informal governance is usually just hierarchy and urgency. That is not governance. That is survival.

A common fix is a simple steering structure with real executive sponsorship. Not a symbolic sponsor who shows up once a year, but a leader who expects updates, asks hard questions, and supports the operational changes that risk reduction requires. When leaders treat risk like a performance topic, it becomes one. When they treat it like a compliance topic, it becomes paperwork.

Translate the strategy into "what changes on Monday?"

Strategies fail because they do not tell people what to do differently. They describe what the organization wants, not what the organization will practice.

This is where risk leaders need to become translators. If the strategy says, "improve risk culture," what does that mean for a supervisor? It might mean pre-task briefings on high-risk work. It might mean coaching conversations that address shortcuts without humiliating people. It might mean reporting near misses without fear of retaliation. It might mean stopping work when conditions change.

If the strategy says, "strengthen third-party risk," what changes in procurement? It might mean a standardized risk review for high-risk contracts, clear insurance requirements, vendor incident notification timelines, and documented safety responsibilities.

If the strategy says, "be data-driven," what changes in meetings? It might mean reviewing leading indicators, not only injury counts. It might mean tracking corrective actions to closure and verifying in the field. It might mean treating reporting quality as a metric, so you can detect underreporting.

Deming's work on quality improvement is still helpful here because it insists that management's job is to improve the system, not just demand better outcomes (Deming, 1986). When you translate strategy into system changes, people can follow. When you translate strategy into slogans, people ignore it.

A good test is this: can a frontline supervisor explain the strategy in one minute using plain language, and describe two specific behaviors that will change this month? If not, the strategy is not ready for implementation.

Build a cadence that makes follow-through unavoidable

Implementation is mostly follow-up. If follow-up is optional, the program becomes optional.

The best implementation cadence is boring in the best way. It repeats. It is predictable. It does not depend on one charismatic leader.

A practical cadence has three layers.

First is the weekly layer where supervisors touch risk in real work. That might be a short safety huddle, a hazard scan, a coaching conversation, or a quick review of open corrective actions. This is where risk becomes normal.

Second is the monthly layer where department leaders review performance signals and make decisions. This is where trends are noticed and resources get assigned.

Third is the quarterly layer where executives review enterprise-level risk themes, cross-department dependencies, and whether the strategy is actually moving. This is where priorities are protected and tradeoffs are made visible.

This is not about creating a calendar full of meetings. It is about creating a rhythm where the same few questions are asked repeatedly until the organization improves. PDSA, or Plan-Do-Study-Act, is useful as a mental model because it keeps implementation tied to learning rather than perfection (Deming, 1986). If you do not study results and adjust, you are not implementing, you are performing.

Adoption is the hard part, not the rollout

Many organizations confuse rollout with implementation. They announce a program, deliver training, publish a policy, and consider it "done." Then they are surprised when behavior does not change.

Change management research has been consistent about this: change requires more than information. It requires reinforcement, local ownership, and the removal of barriers (Kotter, 1996; Hiatt, 2006). People may agree with the change and still not adopt it if it adds friction to their day or threatens their identity.

If you want adoption, build it in.

Make the desired behaviors easier than the workarounds.
Give supervisors scripts and tools that fit their day.

Clarify what good looks like through examples, not just policy language.
Reinforce early wins quickly, especially when staff report hazards or near misses.
Train leaders to respond with curiosity before judgment, so reporting stays alive.

Psychological safety matters here, not as a feel-good concept, but as a control issue. If people fear blame or retaliation, they stop reporting problems. When reporting stops, leaders lose early warning and risk becomes reactive (Edmondson, 1999). Risk leaders should pay attention to whether the organization is safe to tell the truth. That is one of the strongest predictors of whether a strategy will become real.

Put measurement to work, and do not let it lie to you

Measurement is not a scoreboard. It is a steering wheel.

But measurement can also distort behavior. If you reward low incident numbers without checking reporting health, people learn to hide incidents. Underreporting is not rare. It is a predictable response to punitive systems (Probst & Estrada, 2010). If you measure only training completion, you get sign-in sheets. If you measure only inspections completed, you get shallow inspections. People respond to what the system rewards.

A better approach is a balanced measurement set that includes lagging indicators, leading indicators, and indicators of learning.

Lagging indicators tell you what happened: claims, severity, litigation, lost time, and cost trends.
Leading indicators tell you what is building: hazard correction timeliness, corrective action closure, preventive maintenance completion, supervisor coaching frequency, and near-miss reporting trends.
Learning indicators tell you whether the system is improving: repeated hazards, repeat incident types, time to implement corrective actions, and whether fixes hold over time.

This aligns with how serious safety organizations think about leading and lagging indicators and the need to prevent "drift" into normalizing risk (Hopkins, 2009; Vaughan, 1996). It also aligns with high-reliability thinking, which focuses on sensitivity to operations and learning before the big failure occurs (Weick & Sutcliffe, 2001).

If you want measurement that leaders trust, normalize by exposure. Compare rates with context, such as hours worked, miles driven, work orders completed, patient days, or student contact hours. Also, validate data quality. A low incident rate can mean improvement, or it can mean silence. If reporting drops when workloads rise, that is a signal. Risk leaders should treat it as one.

Implementation lives in the middle managers and supervisors

A strategy can have executive support and still fail if supervisors are not equipped. Supervisors are where risk decisions happen in real time: whether to stop work, whether to push a timeline, whether to accept a workaround, whether to coach or ignore, and whether to document properly.

This is why capability building is not optional. Training needs to be less about rules and more about judgment. Supervisors need to practice conversations, not just hear about them. They need to know how to respond when someone reports a hazard. They need to know how to conduct a meaningful post-incident review without turning it into blame. They need to understand what "reasonable" looks like in documentation.

Reason's work on human error and system defenses is useful here because it highlights that incidents usually involve multiple layers of failure, not a single bad actor (Reason, 1997). Supervisors should be trained to look for system contributors: workload, equipment, clarity, staffing, design, and competing incentives. That approach improves learning and reduces repeat events.

If your strategy relies on supervisors but does not support them, your strategy is built on hope.

A practical implementation model: the 90-day cycle

Organizations often want multi-year roadmaps. That is fine, but implementation moves faster when you work in 90-day cycles. Ninety days is long enough to change something real and short enough to maintain urgency.

A solid 90-day cycle has four steps.

First, pick a small number of priorities tied to your highest risk drivers. Not ten. A few.

Second, define what will change operationally. Who will do what differently, where, and when?

Third, track progress weekly and remove barriers quickly. If procurement blocks the change, fix procurement. If staffing blocks the change, address staffing. If training blocks the change, redesign training.

Fourth, review outcomes at the end of the cycle and decide what to standardize, what to adjust, and what to stop. That is continuous improvement in practice (Deming, 1986; Juran & Godfrey, 1999).

This approach protects you from a common trap: launching too many initiatives and finishing none. It also builds credibility because people can see tangible change in a predictable time frame.

Case example: from "risk plan" to operational change in a public agency

Consider a mid-sized public agency with recurring vehicle incidents, strained field operations, and rising claim severity. Leadership approves a risk strategy that includes training, inspections, and improved reporting. The documents look solid. The outcomes do not change.

A closer look shows why. Training is delivered, but supervisors do not reinforce it, and staff do not see changes in equipment or scheduling. Inspections occur, but corrective actions sit open for months because no one has the authority to prioritize them against other work. Reporting is encouraged, but employees do not trust that reporting will be met with learning rather than discipline.

Implementation begins when governance is clarified. Department heads are assigned ownership of specific risk drivers, and corrective-action closure becomes a standing agenda item in monthly operations meetings. The agency chooses a 90-day priority: reduce backing-up incidents and strains associated with material handling.

Operational changes follow. Yard layout is adjusted to reduce congestion. Spotter use is standardized in high-risk areas. Material staging is redesigned to reduce repeated lifts. Supervisors receive short coaching tools and expectations for weekly check-ins. Reporting is simplified, and leadership commits to visible feedback, showing what changed as a result of reports.

In 90 days, incident counts are not the only outcome. The bigger shift is that corrective actions start closing, supervisors coach more consistently, and employees see the organization taking hazards seriously. Over time, severity trends begin to improve because conditions improve, not because the organization got better at paperwork.

This is what "plans to practice" looks like. It is not dramatic. It is disciplined.

Sustainment: Do not let the system drift back

Even good implementation decays if it is not maintained. Drift is normal. People revert to old habits under stress. Workarounds creep back in. New supervisors arrive. Priorities shift. This is why sustainment is not a separate phase. It is part of implementation.

High-reliability thinking emphasizes preoccupation with failure and a reluctance to simplify. That does not mean paranoia. It means staying attentive to weak signals and refusing to treat small deviations as normal (Weick & Sutcliffe, 2001). Vaughan's work on normalization of deviance shows how organizations gradually accept higher risk when nothing bad happens immediately (Vaughan, 1996). Those patterns show up in everyday operations all the time.

Sustainment requires a few consistent mechanisms: periodic verification that controls are used in the field, internal audits that focus on reality, not just documents, management reviews that ask whether the strategy is changing outcomes, and a habit of refreshing training and expectations when conditions change (ISO, 2018).

It also requires something simple: leaders have to keep asking for evidence. Not as a "gotcha," but as a way to keep the system honest. Are corrective actions actually closed? Are hazards being corrected faster or slower? Are we seeing repeat incident types? Are we losing the reporting signal? Are we making exceptions that are becoming permanent?

When those questions stop, drift starts.

Closing

Implementing a risk strategy is mostly about turning ideas into routines and routines into habits. The strategy matters, but execution is where trust is built. People watch what leaders follow up on, what leaders fund, and what leaders tolerate. They decide whether the strategy is real based on those signals, not based on the document.

If you want to pressure-test your implementation, try two reflections. First, if a new supervisor started tomorrow, could they quickly understand what matters in risk and what their role is, without reading a 60-page plan? Second, if you removed the risk manager from the organization for 60 days, would the system keep running, or would it stall? The answers tell you whether you have a program or whether you have a person holding it together.

Good implementation is not glamorous. It is repeatable. It is visible. It makes risk decisions easier to defend because the organization can show its method, not just its intention. That is how plans become practice.

References

COSO. (2017). *Enterprise risk management: Integrating with strategy and performance.* Committee of Sponsoring Organizations of the Treadway Commission.

Deming, W. E. (1986). *Out of the crisis.* MIT Press.

Edmondson, A. (1999). Psychological safety and learning behavior in work teams. *Administrative Science Quarterly, 44*(2), 350–383.

Hiatt, J. (2006). *ADKAR: A model for change in business, government and our community.* Prosci.

Hopkins, A. (2009). Thinking about process safety indicators. *Safety Science, 47*(4), 460–465.

ISO. (2018). *ISO 31000:2018 Risk management — Guidelines.* International Organization for Standardization.

Juran, J. M., & Godfrey, A. B. (1999). *Juran's quality handbook* (5th ed.). McGraw-Hill.

Kotter, J. P. (1996). *Leading change.* Harvard Business School Press.

Probst, T. M., & Estrada, A. X. (2010). Accident under-reporting among employees: Testing the moderating influence of psychological safety climate and supervisor enforcement of safety practices. *Accident Analysis & Prevention, 42*(5), 1438–1444.

Reason, J. (1997). *Managing the risks of organizational accidents.* Ashgate.

Simon, H. A. (1955). A behavioral model of rational choice. *The Quarterly Journal of Economics, 69*(1), 99–118.

Vaughan, D. (1996). *The Challenger launch decision: Risky technology, culture, and deviance at NASA.* University of Chicago Press.

Weick, K. E., & Sutcliffe, K. M. (2001). *Managing the unexpected: Assuring high performance in an age of complexity.* Jossey-Bass.

Chapter 20
The Risk Manager Is Becoming a Translator

Bridging Strategy, Operations, and Human Decision-Making

Introduction: The Risk Manager Is Becoming a Translator

Most leaders do not wake up wanting to talk about risk. They want to meet service levels, finish projects, keep people staffed, stay within budget, and avoid embarrassment in public. They are not deliberately avoiding risk management. They are reacting to everything else that feels louder and more urgent.

That is precisely why the future risk leader has to be a translator.

A modern risk manager translates between worlds that do not always trust each other. Operations speak in deadlines, staffing, productivity, and public expectations. Finance speaks in forecasts, reserves, and constraints. HR speaks in people, behavior, and policy. Legal speaks in exposure and defensibility. IT speaks in systems, vulnerabilities, and uptime. Frontline employees speak in reality: what is happening, what is breaking down, and what is being ignored.

The old version of the role tried to own the conversation. The new version makes the conversation possible. It connects the dots, keeps the message grounded, and helps decision-makers see second- and third-order impacts before they become tomorrow's crises.

If this book has argued anything, it is this: risk management only works when it becomes part of how the organization thinks, not just what the organization documents. The future is not about more forms. It is about better decisions.

What Is Driving the Shift

The job is changing because the environment is changing. Most organizations are dealing with more complexity, faster change, and less margin for error. A few forces keep showing up, regardless of industry.

Risk is moving faster than annual planning cycles.

Cyber events, supply chain disruptions, workforce instability, misinformation, extreme weather, and public scrutiny can turn a normal week into a high-consequence week. Many risks do not give you a slow warning. They show up as a sudden demand for decisions.

Costs are harder to hide.

Claims costs, turnover costs, overtime costs, litigation costs, and reputation costs pile up quickly. Public agencies feel it through council pressure and tight budgets. Private organizations feel it through margins and insurance markets. Either way, "we cannot afford this" is becoming the most common risk conversation in the room.

Regulators are increasing expectations, but not doing the work for you.

Laws and standards keep expanding, but compliance still depends on your internal habits. Policies are not protection if the organization does not live by them.

Work is more public than it used to be.

A single incident can become a headline. A complaint can go viral. A bad decision can become a public trust issue. In many workplaces, reputation risk is no longer a public relations topic. It is an operations topic.

Technology is raising the ceiling and the stakes.

Data systems, sensors, automation, and AI can reduce risk, but they can also introduce new failure modes. The future risk manager cannot treat technology like someone else's problem. It is now part of the risk landscape.

The New Job Description: From Risk Owner to Risk Architect

One of the most important mindset changes is this: the risk manager is not the owner of risk. They are the architect of risk capability.

Owning risk sounds responsible, but it can quietly weaken the organization. When everyone believes risk lives in one department, the rest of the organization stops building its own instincts. That is how you get managers who do not know their own exposures, supervisors who treat safety as paperwork, and executives who only engage when something goes wrong.

The better model is shared ownership with a clear structure.

The risk leader's job is to design the system that makes shared ownership real. That system includes:

- Clear governance and decision rights
- Simple tools that match how work actually happens
- Honest reporting and learning loops
- Practical training that builds competence, not just attendance
- Metrics that drive action, not performance theater

- A culture where people speak up early without getting punished for it

This is the shift from being the person who collects the information to the person who strengthens the organization's ability to see and act.

The Future Role in Leadership: Being at the Table Without Becoming Political

Many risk managers want a seat at the table, but what they really need is influence in the right moments.

The future of risk leadership is not about being the loudest voice in the room. It is about being trusted when decisions carry risk and tradeoffs. That trust is built through consistency.

You build influence when you can do three things well:

1. Say what matters in plain language.

If leaders cannot repeat the risk issue back in their own words, the risk message did not land. The goal is clarity, not technical credibility.

2. Offer options, not just warnings.

Leaders get numb to "we should not do this." They respond to choices. The future risk leader frames the decision and shows the tradeoffs, including what happens if the organization does nothing.

3. Stay steady under pressure.

In a crisis, people look for emotional stability as much as technical guidance. The risk manager who panics, postures, or turns everything into blame loses credibility quickly. The one who stays calm, gathers facts, and helps the team prioritize becomes essential.

Risk leadership is not about controlling leaders. It is about helping leaders make decisions they can defend, operationally and ethically.

Risk Management as Culture Work

The future of risk management is inseparable from culture, because risk is inseparable from behavior.

Most incidents are not caused by one bad person. They come from patterns: shortcuts that become normal, silence that becomes habit, workload that becomes chronic, and leadership signals that become permission.

In practice, culture work is not motivational speaking. It is operational.

It looks like:

- Supervisors correcting unsafe practices early, consistently, and respectfully

- Leaders following through when employees raise concerns

- Teams learning from near misses without turning it into a hunt for someone to blame

- Managers budgeting for maintenance and training instead of treating them like optional extras

- Meetings that are built for decisions and accountability, not updates and performance

If the organization's culture rewards speed over quality, silence over honesty, and blame over learning, you will keep paying for it. The future risk manager is the person who helps leaders see those cultural costs clearly and then helps them change what is being rewarded.

The Risk Manager as a Systems Thinker

The future role requires systems thinking, because risk rarely sits inside one department.

A workplace violence incident is not only a security issue. It is training, communication, reporting, supervision, environmental design, staffing, and post-incident support.

A serious vehicle loss is not only a driver issue. It is policies, scheduling, fatigue, maintenance, routing, discipline, and leadership tolerance for shortcuts.

A workers' compensation spike is not only a claims issue. It is job design, staffing, modified-duty availability, supervisor behavior, medical management, and trust.

A data breach is not only an IT issue. It is training, access controls, vendor management, leadership expectations, and how the organization handles exceptions.

The risk manager of the future has to see these chains. They have to ask the second question, not just the first one. They have to connect early warning signals across departments and help leaders take action before the organization pays the full price.

Data, AI, and the New Accountability

Technology will continue to expand, but accountability is not going away. If anything, it is tightening.

Data and analytics are becoming expected. Dashboards, predictive indicators, and automated reporting can reduce blind spots. But there are two traps that the future risk leader must avoid.

Trap one: confusing data with truth.

Data is only as good as the inputs, the definitions, and the incentives behind it. If supervisors underreport near misses to look better, your "improvement" is fake. If departments code incidents differently, your trends are noise. If the dashboard makes people feel punished, it will make the data worse.

Trap two: automating bad decisions.

AI and automation can increase efficiency, but they can also scale mistakes. If you build a model on messy data and treat it like an answer machine, you will create confidence without competence. The risk leader needs to push for governance: who owns the model, how it is monitored, what decisions it can influence, and what humans still must verify.

The most important future skill is not "using AI." It is knowing where AI helps, where it harms, and how to keep decisions defensible.

The Talent Shift: Risk Leaders Will Need Range

The old pathway into risk management often emphasized technical expertise first. The future still needs technical ability, but it also demands range.

Risk professionals will need to be competent in:

- Communication and facilitation
- Basic finance and budgeting logic

- Claims and litigation realities

- Safety systems and human behavior

- Cyber and technology fundamentals

- Training and adult learning

- Crisis leadership and recovery

- Governance and ethics

This does not mean one person must be an expert in everything. It means the risk leader must be able to hold conversations across disciplines and build partnerships without getting dismissed.

The future also demands stronger succession planning. Too many organizations rely on a single risk leader who holds the history in their head. When that person leaves, the program collapses into compliance mode again. The future model builds bench strength, documents institutional knowledge, and rotates responsibilities enough that the organization does not become dependent on one voice.

What Leaders Should Expect From Risk in the Next Five Years

You will see more organizations shifting from reactive risk management to integrated risk management, but only if leadership expects it.

That means leaders should expect their risk team to bring:

Earlier signals.

Not just claims data after the fact, but leading indicators that show where controls are weakening.

More cross-department coordination.

Risk work that connects HR, operations, finance, legal, IT, and safety instead of letting each operate in isolation.

Decision support, not just documentation.

Short, clear briefs that give leaders options and consequences.

More focus on resilience.

Plans for disruption, not just prevention. The question becomes "how quickly can we recover and keep operating."

Better measurement of real outcomes.

Not training attendance alone, but whether behavior changed, whether corrective actions stuck, and whether costs moved.

This is the direction the role is heading. The organizations that embrace it will have fewer surprises and better recovery when surprises happen anyway.

A Practical 30-Day Playbook: Reimagining the Role Without Starting a War

If a risk leader wants to move toward this future role, they usually face a constraint: the organization still expects them to do the old job.

So, the first step is not a reorg chart. It is credibility.

Week 1: Clarify what the organization actually wants.

Meet with the top decision makers and ask a simple question: "What risk issue keeps you up at night right now?" Then ask what success would look like in six months. This creates a shared target.

Week 2: Identify one high-leverage risk pattern.

Pick a problem where a slight improvement will matter. It could be a recurring injury type, a claim-handling delay, a vehicle trend, a contract-language gaps, or a reporting breakdown. You are looking for a problem that leaders already recognize.

Week 3: Build a simple decision tool.

Create something leaders can use. A one-page risk brief. A short dashboard. A risk register that is actually prioritized. A training plan that is tied to specific exposures. Make it practical.

Week 4: Deliver one visible win and one long-term proposal.

The visible win builds credibility. The long-term proposal shows direction. The combination helps leaders see that risk management is not just a critique. It is value.

This is how you start reimagining the role without triggering defensiveness. You lead with usefulness.

Conclusion: The Future Is Not More Risk Work, It Is Better Risk Thinking

Risk management is not becoming more important because risk departments are asking for attention. It is becoming more important because organizations cannot afford the old way of operating.

The future risk manager is a translator, a facilitator, a systems thinker, and a trusted advisor. They are not there to scare leaders. They are there to help leaders think clearly, act earlier, and recover faster.

If there is one final idea to leave with, it is this:

Most organizations do not change because they finally find the perfect policy. They change when they finally decide to stop paying the same cost over and over.

Reimagining the role is not about titles. It is about impact. And the organizations that treat risk management as a leadership function, not a compliance function, will be the ones that stay standing when the next disruption hits.

Conclusion: Caring Before Something Happens

If you only take one idea from *Risk Management Reimagined,* let it be this: risk management is not a department. It is a way of thinking and leading that shows up in everyday decisions, especially when time is tight, budgets are stressed, and people are tired. You can feel it in how supervisors run a job, how leaders talk about near misses, how meetings are structured, and how seriously the organization treats follow-through. That is why this book has treated risk work as an organizational philosophy that belongs to everyone, not a technical function that lives in a silo.

You have walked through six connected parts because real risk performance is never one lever. It is an ecosystem.

You started with foundations: assessment and cost control. Assessments only matter when they inform decisions, and cost control only becomes credible when leaders understand what drives frequency, severity, and exposure over time. You then moved into the human core: culture, training, and the everyday destroyers of safety excellence. That section matters because culture will always beat paperwork. You cannot write a policy strong enough to overcome a culture that does not mean what it says.

From there, the book widened to governance and leadership. Reporting lines, role design, and crisis leadership are not "org chart issues." They shape what gets attention, what gets funded, and what gets quietly ignored. In a crisis, that structure either supports clear decisions or becomes part of the problem.

Next came data, technology, and decision-making. This is where many organizations get excited and often get disappointed. Tools can absolutely help, but they do not replace judgment. They amplify whatever culture and discipline you already have. If your organization is honest, curious, and consistent, data and technology make you faster and smarter. If your organization is political, fragmented, or afraid to tell the truth, technology just helps you move bad information around more efficiently.

Then you stepped into the larger landscape: sustainability, ESG pressures, and global interdependence. This part is not about trends for trend's sake. It is about acknowledging that today's risks are entangled. Climate, cyber, workforce pressures, supply chains, and public trust now interact in ways that can turn a "small" issue into a public event quickly.

Finally, you reached the point where most books get vague, but where real change either happens or dies: implementation, measurement, and the future of the profession.

Implementation is not a one time rollout. It is a daily practice that lives in calendars, conversations, and choices about what gets attention and what quietly dies.

That line is not poetry. It is a warning. It is also hope. Because it means you do not need perfect conditions to make progress. You need direction, a few well chosen moves, and the discipline to learn as you go.

Measurement is similar. Many teams avoid it because they think measurement is about turning people into numbers. It is not. At its best, it is three simple commitments: we know where we are starting, we are clear about what success looks like, and we will learn from reality and adjust.

If you build that muscle, you get something bigger than better dashboards. You get a culture that learns faster and responds smarter, which is the real payoff.

And that brings us to the future. The future of risk management is not mainly about new checklists. It is about identity. It is about moving from "compliance police" to strategic partners in value, trust, and resilience.

That shift is already happening in high performing organizations, and it will accelerate because risk is accelerating.

What "reimagined" looks like in real life

A reimagined program is not the one with the thickest manual. It is the one where people can answer three questions clearly.

First: Do we tell the truth here?

That truth shows up in near miss reporting, in how incidents are discussed, and in whether the organization can look at uncomfortable patterns without scapegoating. When employees are afraid to speak up, risk stays hidden until it becomes expensive.

Second: Do we learn, or do we just react?

Learning shows up in what happens after the meeting, not in how confident everyone sounded during it. It shows up in whether corrective actions actually close, whether training improves behavior instead of checking a box, and whether leaders are willing to fix systems instead of blaming individuals for predictable outcomes.

Third: Do we protect people and public trust, or do we mainly protect ourselves?

Risk management is not only about avoiding lawsuits or satisfying regulators. It is about protecting people and public trust.

In the public sector especially, trust is an asset you either build slowly or lose quickly. In the private sector, trust is what customers, regulators, and employees decide you deserve. Either way, it is not optional.

A practical way to finish the book

The most common failure after a book, a training, or a strategic plan is that everyone agrees, and then nothing changes. So here is a simple way to close this work with your leadership team, your safety committee, or your department heads.

Pick one chapter that felt uncomfortably familiar, and then answer these questions honestly:

What do we currently do that gives us the illusion of control, but does not actually reduce risk?

Where are we relying on a heroic individual instead of a reliable system?

Which risks are we willing to tolerate, and have we been honest about that, or are we pretending "zero" while funding "barely enough"?

If we improved only one routine in the next 30 days, which routine would create the biggest downstream impact? A meeting cadence, a supervisory walkthrough, a return to work practice, a claims review rhythm, a training reset, a vendor control, a dashboard that leaders actually use.

Who owns follow-through, and how will we know, not hope, that it happened?

That is where the book becomes real. Not in your ability to quote it, but in your ability to convert it into routines.

A final word about the kind of risk leader this era needs

This book has argued that good risk work saves money. Done well, it reduces claims, downtime, turnover, and costly surprises. Done poorly, it turns those costs into a permanent line item.

But the deeper point is that risk management is leadership. It is the leadership practice of noticing what others normalize, asking better questions, refusing to let "that's just how it is" become the standard, and building systems that help people do the right thing on their hardest days.

You do not have to predict the future to be ready for it. You have to build organizations that can learn, adapt, and recover quickly.

If your organization can do that, you will not just reduce loss. You will improve performance, protect your people, strengthen trust, and make your workplace the kind of place good employees want to stay.

There is a quote that frames the spirit of this book: "Most organizations don't care much about risk management, until something happens."

My hope for your organization is simple. Care before something happens. Then prove it in what you fund, what you reward, what you tolerate, and what you fix.

Appendix A: Glossary of Key Terms

Use this glossary as a quick translation guide when you are talking with leaders, staff, TPAs, brokers, and auditors. The goal is plain language, not jargon.

A

Accountability (for safety and risk)

Clear expectations for who is responsible for what, how performance will be measured, and what happens when commitments are met or missed. Good accountability focuses on behaviors and systems, not just blame after an incident.

After-Action Review (AAR)

A structured discussion after an event or exercise that asks: What was supposed to happen? What actually happened? Why? What will we do the same or differently next time? The emphasis is on learning, not punishment.

B

Bowtie Analysis

A visual risk assessment method that shows how a central "top event" (loss of control) is connected to threats on the left and consequences on the right, with preventive and mitigating barriers on each side. Useful for explaining major hazards to non-technical audiences.

Business Continuity

The ability of an organization to keep delivering critical services at an acceptable level during and after a disruption (for example, IT outage, natural disaster, labor action). Often supported by business continuity plans (BCPs) and exercises.

C

Claim Frequency

How often claims occur in a period. Usually expressed as claims per 100 full-time equivalents (FTE) or per 200,000 hours worked. Helps show exposure and trends across departments of different sizes.

Claim Severity

How serious claims are once they occur, usually measured by cost (incurred dollars) or impact (lost days, permanent impairment). Frequency and severity together give a clearer picture than either alone.

Corrective Action

A specific step taken to remove a hazard or fix a system weakness identified through an incident, inspection, audit, or risk assessment. Good corrective actions name the owner, the deadline, and how completion will be verified.

Cost of Risk / Total Cost of Risk (TCOR)

The full cost of managing risk, including premiums, retained losses (deductibles and self-insured amounts), claims administration, risk control, and sometimes indirect costs such as overtime, temporary staff, or lost productivity. Often normalized per $1,000 of payroll or revenue.

Culture (Safety / Risk)

"The way we really do things around here" when it comes to safety and risk, not just what policies say. Includes shared assumptions, stories, incentives, and what people believe leadership truly values.

D

Dashboard (Risk or Safety Dashboard)

A visual display of key indicators that provides a quick view of current performance and trends. A good dashboard is tailored to its audience and prompts decisions, not just observation.

Data-Driven Decision Making

Using structured data (claims, incidents, audits, surveys, financials) and clear definitions to guide choices about priorities, staffing, investments, and policies. It complements, rather than replaces, professional judgment and frontline experience.

E

Enterprise Risk Management (ERM)

A coordinated approach to managing all of an organization's risks (strategic, operational, financial, compliance, reputational) in a connected way, rather than in separate silos. Emphasizes alignment with mission, strategy, and performance.

ESG (Environmental, Social, and Governance)

A lens for understanding long-term risks and opportunities related to environmental impact (E), social factors such as equity and labor practices (S), and governance quality (G). Increasingly used by regulators, investors, and communities to judge organizational performance and resilience.

Exposure

The people, assets, activities, or situations that could be affected by a risk event (for example, fleet miles driven, number of employees, square footage of facilities, number of park visitors). Often used to normalize rates and prioritize controls.

F

Failure Modes and Effects Analysis (FMEA)

A structured method for examining how a process, product, or system can fail, what the effects would be, how often failures might occur, and how likely they are to be detected in time. Uses a Risk Priority Number (RPN) to focus attention on the most critical failure modes.

Full-Time Equivalent (FTE)

A standard way to express staffing levels. Typically, one FTE equals one person working full time (for example, 2,080 hours per year). Used to normalize claims and incident rates across different departments or years.

H

Hazard

A source or situation with the potential to cause harm to people, property, or the environment (for example, unguarded machinery, wet floors, high-speed traffic, poorly secured data).

Hierarchy of Controls

A ranked approach to risk control: eliminate the hazard, substitute something safer, use engineering controls, then administrative controls (policies, procedures), and finally personal protective equipment (PPE). The higher levels (elimination and substitution) are more effective than relying only on PPE.

I

Incident

Any unplanned event that results in, or could have resulted in, injury, illness, property damage, service disruption, or reputational impact. Includes both actual losses and near misses, depending on reporting practices.

Incident Investigation

A structured process for understanding what happened, why it happened, and what changes are needed to prevent recurrence. Good investigations look at system and organizational factors, not just "who made a mistake."

Injury and Illness Prevention Program (IIPP)

In jurisdictions like California, a required written program that outlines responsibility, hazard identification, training, communication, and correction for workplace safety and health. The IIPP is the backbone of many safety systems.

ISO 31000

A widely used international standard that provides principles and guidelines for risk management. Emphasizes integrating risk thinking into strategy, decision-making, and daily operations.

J

Job Hazard Analysis (JHA) / Job Safety Analysis (JSA)

A method that breaks a job or task into steps, identifies hazards at each step, and defines controls before work begins. Best used for high-risk, complex, or new tasks.

L

Lagging Indicator

A measure of events that have already happened (injuries, claims, serious incidents, lost days). Helpful for tracking outcomes and trends, but not for predicting what will happen next on its own.

Leading Indicator

A measure of behaviors, conditions, or activities that tend to precede events (near-miss reports, hazard inspections, training completion, corrective action closure). Leading indicators are used to anticipate and prevent problems.

Loss Time / Lost-Time Injury

An injury or illness that results in one or more days away from work beyond the day of the event. Often tracked separately from medical-only cases as a sign of more severe outcomes.

M

Mitigation (Risk Mitigation)

Actions taken to reduce the likelihood or impact of a risk event. Mitigation can include design changes, training, additional staffing, system improvements, or contractual risk transfer.

Moral Hazard

A situation where one party is more likely to take risks because another party bears most of the consequences (for example, insured entities taking less care because they feel fully protected by insurance).

N

Near Miss / Close Call

An unplanned event that did not result in injury, damage, or loss, but had the potential to do so if circumstances had been slightly different. Near misses are rich learning opportunities when reported and analyzed.

P

PDCA (Plan–Do–Check–Act)

A simple continuous improvement cycle: plan a change, implement it, check the results, and act based on what you learned (adopt, adapt, or abandon). Widely used in quality, safety, and risk improvement work.

Psychological Safety

A shared belief that the team is safe for interpersonal risk taking. In a psychologically safe environment, people feel comfortable speaking up about mistakes, concerns, and ideas without fear of humiliation or retaliation. Critical for effective reporting and learning.

Pure Risk vs. Speculative Risk

Pure risks involve the potential for loss or no loss (for example, fire, injury). Speculative risks involve the potential for loss or gain (for example, investments, strategic moves). Organizational risk management must address both.

R

Residual Risk

The level of risk that remains after controls and mitigations have been applied. No system can eliminate all risk; residual risk must be understood, accepted, or further reduced.

Risk Appetite

The amount and type of risk an organization is willing to pursue or retain in pursuit of its objectives. Often set by elected officials, boards, or executives and used to guide decisions.

Risk Assessment

A process for identifying risks, analyzing their likelihood and impact, and prioritizing them for treatment. Can be qualitative (low/medium/high) or quantitative (numeric scores, probabilities, dollar values).

Risk Priority Number (RPN)

A numeric score used in FMEA, calculated by multiplying ratings for severity (S), occurrence (O), and detection (D):

RPN = S × O × D.

Higher numbers indicate failure modes that deserve more attention.

Risk Register

A living list of identified risks, with information on their causes, potential impacts, owners, current controls, and planned actions. Used as a central reference for risk discussion and tracking.

Risk Tolerance

The specific level of variation around objectives that an organization is willing to accept. Often more granular than appetite (for example, acceptable ranges for injury rates, budget variance, or service downtime).

S

Safety Culture

The shared values, beliefs, and behaviors that shape how people think and act about safety at work. It shows up in what is rewarded, ignored, or punished when no one is watching.

SC³ (Safety Cultural Competence Continuum)

The framework in this book that describes stages of safety culture maturity: Safety Cultural Destructiveness, Incapacity, Blindness, Pre-Competence, Competence, and Proficiency. Used to diagnose where you are and plan realistic next steps.

Scorecard

A structured set of metrics for a department or function that includes targets, current performance, and brief notes on actions. More narrative than a dashboard and often used in regular reviews with leaders.

Stakeholder

Any person or group affected by, or able to affect, an organization's activities and risk decisions (for example, employees, residents, elected officials, unions, regulators, vendors).

T

Telematics

Technology used to monitor vehicle or equipment location and behavior (speed, harsh braking, rapid acceleration, idle time). Used to manage fleet risk, coach drivers, and improve fuel and maintenance performance.

Total Recordable Injury Rate (TRIR)

A standard injury-rate metric used to compare injury frequency over time or between organizations of different sizes:

TRIR = (Number of OSHA recordable cases × 200,000) ÷ total hours worked.

The factor 200,000 represents 100 full-time employees working 2,000 hours per year.

W

Workers' Compensation (WC)

The statutory system that provides medical benefits and wage replacement to employees injured in the course of employment, typically in exchange for limits on lawsuits against the employer. WC is a major cost driver and a central focus of many public-sector risk programs.

Workplace Violence (WPV)

Any act or threat of physical violence, harassment, intimidation, or other threatening, disruptive behavior that occurs at the work site or in connection with work. Increasingly regulated, with specific prevention-plan requirements in many jurisdictions.

References – Glossary

These sources inform several of the definitions above and the overall approach to risk and safety used in this book.

- Edmondson, A. C. (2019). *The fearless organization: Creating psychological safety in the workplace for learning, innovation, and growth*. Wiley.

- Hollnagel, E. (2014). *Safety-I and Safety-II: The past and future of safety management*. Ashgate.

- International Electrotechnical Commission. (2019). *IEC 60812:2019: Analysis techniques for system reliability – Procedure for failure mode and effects analysis (FMEA)*. Author.

- International Organization for Standardization. (2018). *ISO 31000:2018 Risk management – Guidelines*. Author.

- National Institute for Occupational Safety and Health. (2015). *Hierarchy of controls*. Centers for Disease Control and Prevention.

- Occupational Safety and Health Administration. (2012). *OSHA recordkeeping handbook*. U.S. Department of Labor.

Appendix B: Safety Cultural Competency Continuum (SC³) Model

SAFETY CULTURAL COMPETENCY CONTINUUM MODEL

Components	Safety Cultural Destructiveness	Safety Cultural Incapacity	Safety Cultural Blindness	Safety Cultural Pre-Competence	Safety Cultural Competence	Safety Cultural Proficiency
Leadership Commitment to Safety	Disregard safety entirely, seeing it as a "cost of doing business."	Safety messaging is inconsistent and superficial	Assume all employees share the same safety values without actively reinforcing them.	Recognize the importance of safety but struggle to align it with operational goals.	Consistently emphasize safety as a core value.	Actively champion safety innovation and improvement.
Employee Involvement	Feedback is ignored, and dissenting voices are silenced.	Aware of safety policies but feel discouraged or powerless to contribute.	Follow safety procedures only to meet quotas. Safety feedback is solicited but not acted upon.	Encouraged to participate, but mechanisms for involvement are underdeveloped.	Actively participate in safety programs and provide regular feedback	Lead safety initiatives and mentor peers in safety best practices
Training and Competence	Non-existent or inadequate training on safety protocols	Exists but is outdated, inconsistent, or irrelevant,	Generic and assumes all employees share the same safety needs	Programs developed but not fully integrated into operations.	Effectiveness is regularly evaluated and improved.	Dynamic, updated continuously, focus on emerging risks.
Accountability	No one is held accountable for unsafe practices.	Accountability measures are nonexistent, or selectively applied	Accountability is only addressed in response to major incidents	Accountability measures are introduced but not fully implemented.	Clear account-ability structures in place, performance regularly reviewed.	Embedded into the organization's culture, with shared outcome ownership
Communication	Safety communication is absent or actively suppressed.	Inconsistent or unclear messaging, sporadic and doesn't meet needs	Safety messages are generic and fail to address specific needs	Leaders begin to solicit feedback but struggle with follow-through	Consistent, clear, and emphasizes relevance to team	Fosters open dialogue, feedback and culture of trust
Measurement and Feedback	Safety performance is not measured at all.	Metrics are collected inconsistently or only for compliance.	Metrics focused solely on lagging indicators such as incident rates	Metrics are developed but no integration with operational goals	Data is used to drive improvements.	Feedback drives innovation and strategic planning.
Integration with Organizational Goals	Safety goals actively undermined to prioritize production.	Integration efforts are superficial or non-existent.	Safety in planning but not fully integrated operations	Safety included in planning but not consistently prioritized	Safety embedded into strategic and operational plans.	Core organizational value, fully integrated
Continuous Improvement	Resistant to change and perpetuates unsafe practices.	Improvements are reactive rather than proactive.	Change is seen as unnecessary or burdensome.	Initiatives are launched but inconsistently implemented.	Organizational priority with regular updates.	Model of safety excellence in its industry.

Modified from "The Cultural Competence Continuum" by Cross, T. L., Bazron, B. J., Isaacs, M. R., & Dennis, K. W. (1989) in collaboration with Dr. Lamar Jerome Smith in 2014.

Appendix C: The SC³ Supporting Documents:

A Quick Orientation

SC³ is a practical framework for understanding why risk outcomes differ between organizations that appear similar on paper.

It focuses on patterns of decisions under pressure, not on slogans, intentions, or isolated events.

SC³ examines three interacting elements:

Systems
The processes, tools, handoffs, technology, staffing, and structures that shape how work actually gets done.

Cognition
How people perceive risk, make decisions, manage attention, and operate under time pressure, fatigue, and competing demands.

Culture
What the organization truly values, rewards, tolerates, and ignores — especially when no one is watching.

Most serious failures are not caused by a single mistake or a single person. They emerge when weaknesses in systems, predictable human limitations, and cultural signals align.

SC³ helps teams stop asking only "Who failed?" and start asking:

- What conditions made this outcome likely?
- What signals did we miss?
- Where did our systems, assumptions, or incentives work against us?

SC³ as a Mirror and a Roadmap

SC³ is not a scorecard or a maturity label. It is a way to structure better conversations and better decisions.

Used honestly, it serves two purposes:

A mirror
It helps organizations see their current patterns clearly — including gaps between stated values and day-to-day practice.

A roadmap

It points to realistic next steps for improvement, one stage at a time, without requiring perfection.

SC^3 is applied in practical ways:

- Snapshot assessments to establish a shared baseline
- Evidence checks to reduce opinion-driven debates
- Dashboards and scorecards that support decisions, not just reporting
- Action tracking tools that make ownership visible

You do not need perfect data or sophisticated software to use SC^3. You need clarity, discipline, and a willingness to look honestly at how work actually happens.

SC^3 Component Rating – How to Score

This rating is meant to reveal patterns, not produce a single "culture score."

Use these guidelines:

- It is normal to land in different stages across components.
- If you are debating between two stages, choose the lower one.
- A single strong department does not move the whole organization.

Common traps to avoid

- Rating based on policies rather than practice
- Letting one recent success overshadow repeated issues
- Confusing activity (training held, meetings scheduled) with impact

After rating, look for clusters:

- Which components sit earlier on the continuum?
- Which ones appear more developed?
- Where are the gaps most likely to create risk?

These patterns will guide which tools you use to improve.

SC³ Quick Snapshot

This snapshot is a fast way to surface how your organization currently manages safety and risk; not in theory, but in day-to-day practice.

Do not overthink this page. Your goal is not precision; it is alignment.

Complete this snapshot individually first, then compare responses as a group. Differences in ratings are often more informative than the averages.

Rule: Rate based on what typically happens on a *busy, pressured day*, not on best intentions or written policy.

SC³ Snapshot Table

Component	Destructive	Incapable	Blind	Pre-Competent	Competent	Proficient
Leadership commitment	☐	☐	☐	☐	☐	☐
Employee voice & involvement	☐	☐	☐	☐	☐	☐
Training & competence	☐	☐	☐	☐	☐	☐
Accountability & just response	☐	☐	☐	☐	☐	☐
Communication & information flow	☐	☐	☐	☐	☐	☐
Measurement & feedback	☐	☐	☐	☐	☐	☐
Integration with goals & planning	☐	☐	☐	☐	☐	☐
Learning & continuous improvement	☐	☐	☐	☐	☐	☐

SC³ Component Rating – How to Score

This rating is meant to reveal patterns, not produce a single "culture score."

Use these guidelines:

- It is normal to land in different stages across components.

- If you are debating between two stages, choose the lower one.

- A single strong department does not move the whole organization.

Common traps to avoid

- Rating based on policies rather than practice

- Letting one recent success overshadow repeated issues

- Confusing activity (training held, meetings scheduled) with impact

After rating, look for clusters:

- Which components sit earlier on the continuum?

- Which ones appear more developed?

- Where are the gaps most likely to create risk?

These patterns will guide which tools you use to improve.

www.ingramcontent.com/pod-product-compliance
Lightning Source LLC
Chambersburg PA
CBHW080402270326
41927CB00015B/3327